Pilgrimage to Paris

The Cheapo Snob's Guide to the City and the
Americans Who Lived There

To Chris, Lauren, and the girls —
Get to Paris — you'll love
it! Jayne

Jayne R. Boisvert

Published by Open Books

Copyright © 2018 by Jayne R. Boisvert

Cover images © RossHelen and Olga_C/Shutterstock.com

Interior design by Siva Ram Maganti

ISBN-13: 978-1948598118

To Ray—for his love, support, and advice

Contents

Preface

EVER HEAR OF SOMEONE having "champagne tastes on a beer budget?" Have you often thought that the expression describes you? Do you want to get the best out of life at the most reasonable prices? If so, you are a Cheapo Snob and this guidebook is for you. Who is it not for? Well, probably not for the backpacking, hostel-staying youngster you might once have been. Nor for the "cost is no object" type who sleeps in five-star hotels and goes to Michelin-starred restaurants every night. No, this is for most of the rest of us who are always aiming at the right mix of high standards and affordable costs. Cheapo Snobs take charge of their itinerary, go where they want, when they want. Of course, this kind of lifestyle requires time and perseverance but it can lead to wonderful adventures to fit nearly any budget. Like most big cities, Paris can be quite expensive. Well, let's face it: it IS expensive. Still, there are many free and low-cost options in the City of Light. This guide will tell you about some of the best of them and will help you to find your way. Keeping the Snob dimension in mind, this guide will also highlight a few splurges that might just be up your alley. More importantly, we will look at a new way to explore the city, one which will not only give you a real feel for Paris but will allow you to follow in the footsteps of famous Americans who have lived there. And what a diverse and wonderful group it is: Thomas Jefferson *and* Jim Morrison, James Whistler *and* Isadora Duncan, *and* Julia Child, *and* Archie MacLeish, *and* T.S. Eliot, *and* James Baldwin, *and* well, as you can see, the list is quite long. Reading this guide, you will learn not only about the charming city of Paris, but about the great variety of Americans who for at least part of their lives called it home. What could be cheaper and allow for more bragging rights than exploring the streets of the French capital while visiting the addresses where famous Americans lived, worked, and played?

Leaving no stone unturned, the guide helps you get ready for your trip. Chapter 1 gives a few short tips on finding flights as well as essentials about how and what to pack. Information is included on where to stay and eat, how to get around the city, and how to pay using credit and debit cards. The guide also doesn't overlook the ever-important not so obvious process of finding restrooms in the city. In Chapter 2 the focus is on the best free and nearly free things to do in Paris—walks, parks, museums at no cost, and, perhaps surprisingly to some readers, cemeteries. The twelve *don't-miss* places to see in and around the French capital—from Notre-Dame and the Louvre to Giverny and Versailles—make up the third chapter. Then we begin taking a look at famous Americans who once called Paris home. Chapters 4, 5, and 6 are devoted to writers of fiction, our biggest category by far. You no doubt know that Hemingway and Fitzgerald lived for a while in Paris, but you might just be surprised that authors like Mark Twain, Edith Wharton, William Faulkner, and Saul Bellow, among scores of others, spent time there as well. But the list of Americans in Paris is not just composed of poets, dramatists, and novelists. Chapters 7 through 11 introduce lots of others: journalists, publishers, and critics; politicians; artists and architects; musicians and performers; as well as a "hard-to-classify" category of people who are, well, hard to classify. The information will not only provide a unique way to explore Paris but will introduce you to (or help you recall) these people and why they are considered important. Perhaps even opening you up to new books and explorations once you get back home. A final chapter focuses on the principal cafés in Montparnasse and Saint-Germain, hang-outs associated with these celebrated Americans in years past. Stepping into these cafés today provides a nice way to cap off a visit for Cheapo Snobs wishing to relax and follow in some pretty amazing footsteps.

Chapter 1

Travel Tips

You experienced travelers or armchair visitors out there might not be looking for help with the practical side of traveling. So, if you're eager to learn about a long list of Americans who at one time called Paris home, feel free to skip ahead to the first group of fiction writers in Chapter 4. For others, before exploring the Parisian haunts of our compatriots, we have to get you there first. Here are a few tips that will help in organizing your trip.

Know thyself

A good Cheapo Snob knows when to go Cheapo and when to go Snob. Knowing your bottom line in terms of creature comforts (your "Snob" side) is probably the most important consideration before making any reservations. Your "Cheapo" side might drool over the price of a multi-stopover series of flights—say, Newark-Stockholm-Amsterdam-Paris. This frugal aspect might draw your attention to one-star hotels off the beaten path as well. The "Snob" in you might be willing to compromise as long as it gets to visit all of its must-see sights. For someone else, the "Snob" side might insist on better hotels…or for more convenient flights…or both. Know yourself. Planning will then be that much easier. Realizing that the Cheapo/Snob mix will be different for different folks, this guide's approach is to give ideas on how to find what suits your needs and desires. Instead of specific suggestions of what airlines to pick, which hotels or restaurants to choose, it offers some of the best ways you can design specific travel plans yourself. Here are a few ideas to help you have the time of your life getting to and staying in the French capital while satisfying both your Cheapo and Snob sides.

The Secret to Cheap Airline Fares: There is No Secret

Flights and Luggage: Booking a cheap flight to Europe presents the greatest challenge. Savvy travelers know about the tried and true tips that follow.

- If you can be flexible about your dates of travel, you will find better deals.

- Book your trip outside of the summer months if at all possible. May through September is the most expensive travel time. If your schedule allows you to go in either April or October, you'll find mild temperatures, diminished crowds, and more reasonable prices.

- The optimal period to book your travel is two to three months ahead of your departure date.

- Check websites often and keep track of the rates as you find them. Compare prices on all of the major travel sites: Bing Travel, Cheapoair (got to like the name!), Expedia, Kayak, Momondo, Orbitz, Travelocity, and Routehappy. Google Flights and Price-line each allow you to compare prices on the major travel sites. Hipmunk does the same thing and, as a bonus for your "Snob" side, includes the crucial "agony" factor: the overall length of the flight plus any layover you would have to endure *en route*. Yapta has a notification system which lets you know when flights you're tracking go up or (preferably!) down in price. Armed with this information you'll have a baseline, allowing you to determine what is a good deal.

- Charter flights, which are not so prevalent anymore in the U.S., are usually priced right, but legroom might be tight since they try to squeeze in as many travelers as possible. If you live near major Canadian cities from Vancouver to Montreal, Air Transat could be an option for you.

- You can also visit local travel agents to check out their offerings. For students and faculty who can prove their status, StudentUniverse and STA Travel (for students ages 13 to 26) offer half-price deals on airlines, including Air France! Though it's important to note that STA Travel requires the purchase of an identity card.

- One last idea is to "like" your favorite airline on Facebook. On our last trip to Paris, we got a super deal via Air France after reading their post about having the lowest costs of the season. For once, it was not just a "come-on" but a really great price, believe it or not.

Half the Clothes, Twice the Money

The old aphorism "take half the clothes and twice the money" is true in practically every travel situation. Small carry-on suitcases on wheels (the 14" x 21" or thereabout size) and perhaps a backpack should be the maximum per person, if you can swing it. European cities, including Paris, have lots of stairs, including at train and subway (*métro*) stations. Imagine how difficult these are to navigate when you're lugging hefty bags. Speaking of stairs, another necessity is comfortable shoes. Even if you are catching cabs everywhere, you cannot imagine what a beating your poor feet will take just strolling through parks and museums. The Louvre alone entails eight miles of corridors—though we certainly wouldn't suggest doing all of that in one day or even a week!

Navigating the Stars...Hotel Stars, That Is

Finding a place to stay in the French capital can be easy once you know yourself and understand your Cheapo to Snob ratio. Is a luxury hotel room your top priority? Or do you believe it's just a place to sleep requiring a comfortable bed and clean bathroom? For Cheapos, a two-star hotel is usually sufficient. Keep in mind, however, that if you're in the city in August there may be no air-conditioning at a two-star…talk about the agony factor. Also, it is hard for Americans to believe how tiny Parisian elevators can be, especially in smaller hotels…another reason to pack light. As with airfares, check out lodging by way of the usual suspects on the Web: Expedia, Google Hotel Finder, and Kayak, etc. It's worth paying a visit to the actual hotel website which will sometimes offer substantial reductions on the cost. As a typical big city, Paris has tiny hotel rooms and bathrooms. The less you pay, the less spacious the quarters. Your Cheapo side may approve of the price, but your Snob side might chafe at the creative balancing act required in tight shower stalls.

Find a Home Away from Home

The best all-around option for meeting the needs of the Cheapo and Snob in you is to rent an apartment. Of course, Cheapos will love the savings vis-à-vis hotels. And just think of the reduction in restaurant costs since you will be able to cook as many meals as you want right where you're staying. This will allow your Snob side to enjoy more spacious, comfortable surroundings than in a hotel room and to pay more for nice meals in restaurants whenever it wants. So, how do you go about getting a Parisian apartment? Air BnB, Home Away, or VRBO are good places to start. Stick with well-known services like these to avoid scams and unpleasant surprises. Here are a few things to look for when examining a possible rental:

- Pay attention to the square footage of the apartment (given in square meters which is easy to convert to square feet via the Internet), so that you won't get stuck with impossibly claustrophobic living quarters. By way of comparison, a standard American hotel room measures about 25-30 square meters. So anything that size or larger would probably fit your needs.

- Check to see if there is an elevator in the building (*un ascenseur*). The bad surprise of a tedious climb when first arriving with suitcases might otherwise await. Trust me, we've been there.

- It is also important to note that Europeans calculate floors of a building differently. Our "first floor" is their "ground floor." So, a third-floor apartment, is on what we would call the fourth floor. Okay, so it's just one more flight of stairs, but that might get old fast when you're carrying a heavy load of groceries or when dragging yourself home after an exhausting day of sightseeing.

- Pay attention to the *arrondissement* (district). Central locations bordering the Seine (like in the 4th, 5th, and 6th around the Marais, the Latin Quarter, Saint-Germain, for example) will be quite convenient but will probably be smaller, more expensive, and noisier than if you rent rooms in areas a bit farther out. Say in the 10th or 14th. On the other hand, you might not want to be in the 19th or 20th arrondissement which are quite far from the heart of the city.

- If you happen to be an academic, rentals for professors can be found at www.sabbaticalhomes.com.

Besides the plusses already mentioned, from "your apartment" you will also be able to enjoy a residential neighborhood and to see how the locals live and work.

Getting Around on Land and Water

The way you choose to get to and move around in any big city is once again a question of your Cheapo vs. Snob priorities. For Snobs who value convenience over cost, taxi stands proliferate. Your Cheapo side, however, will undoubtedly balk at the prices. By and large, when frugality dominates, cab rides are reserved for very rare circumstances. Since your first challenge will be getting from the airport to the city, knowing about those options is a good place to start. There are taxis, sure, with a fifty-euro or more price tag. But there are other possibilities. The most Cheapo—though definitely not the most elegant—way to reach the city from the airport is to buy a ticket for about ten euros on the RER. This regional express train is kind of a "super subway," going faster than the regular métro and making fewer stops getting into Paris. From the airport follow signs to RER B and take the CDGVAL—a kind of small train—to the RER station. When you're on the platform, be sure to check out the number of stations the departing train serves. These are listed on the electronic board beside the track. Sometimes waiting a few minutes for a second train with fewer stops will actually get you to your destination much faster.

Another idea is to take a bus. Not a city bus, mind you, but a coach that goes non-stop to the center of the city. For about the same fare as the RER, the Roissybus takes you to the Opéra Garnier on the Right Bank in the 9th arrondissement. Le Bus Direct also called Les Cars Air France (shuttle buses, not cars as the name seems to indicate) depart every half-hour and make stops at place Charles de Gaulle (the location of the Arc de Triomphe where the 8th, 16th, and 17th arrondissements meet), the Gare de Lyon (12th), or the Gare Montparnasse (14th). [http://www.lescarsairfrance.com/en/roissy-cdg-shuttle-bus.html]. For both options, after getting into the city, you may still need to take the métro, another RER, a bus, or a taxi to get to your destination. Not ideal for Snobs, but it's obviously a much better fee all around than taking a cab from the airport.

Once situated downtown, the bus or the métro is the best way to travel; both systems are a terrific way to get around and are relatively user friendly. Buy a *carnet* (small book) of ten tickets at the booth inside the subway for use on either mode of transportation. One advantage of taking the bus is that you can see the city as you travel. Be sure to pay attention to the arrows marked on the bus route maps at each stop since not all round trips take the same roads, usually because of one-way streets. If you're in a hurry, the subway is usually much faster, especially if some demonstration (there are a lot of *manifestations* in Paris) is blocking the bus route. For travel on the métro, you first have to determine the station you want and then look for the last stop on that line. Then simply follow signs within the station for that direction. Some subway cars require you to push a red button or turn a silver handle to get on or off the train. Check what the locals are doing. Follow signs for *Sortie* to find your way out to the street. Another very important thing to do is to keep your ticket handy until you have reached your destination. The exit turnstile may require a ticket. You will also need your ticket when transferring from the métro to the RER. One word of caution: you can transfer subway to subway (including the RER) or bus to bus with just one ticket, but not subway to bus or vice versa. That will require a new ticket.

For a little over 10€, you can buy the subway system's Paris Visite day pass; be sure to purchase them from a reputable source, like in the métro station itself. This would be suitable for those thinking they're going to take seven or more rides a day or would like a price reduction for visiting the top of the Arc de Triomphe, the Tour Montparnasse, or on a ticket to Disneyland Paris. Otherwise, Cheapos will find it's overpriced and not worth the cost.

Another very enjoyable means of getting your bearings in the city is to take a *bateau mouche* ride. These "fly boats" make a loop around the two islands in the Seine—Île de la Cité and Île Saint-Louis—giving visitors a glimpse of the important monuments (like Notre Dame) and an idea of their location. A romantic excursion just before sunset or at night when the lights illuminate the important landmarks is a lovely thing to do for couples and others as well. All of the different companies come in at about the same price with significant reductions for children. I wouldn't trust having meals on board, though, since you'd probably eat much better elsewhere and at a lower cost.

Le Snob Oblige...Certain Things a Snob Just Has to Do

No self-respecting Snob would go to Paris and not visit museums. The Cheapo thus has to figure out how to do this inexpensively, starting with museum passes. Several different types of passes exist which allow you to go to the head of the line at museums: the Paris Museum Pass, Paris City Passport, Paris ComboPass. For convenience, you can't beat them, but you're going to have to pay for that convenience. If you have only a couple of days to spend in the city and have a strong constitution, purchasing one of these passes—usually available for 2, 4, or 6 consecutive days—makes sense. Cost-wise, for example, if you want to see the Louvre and Sainte-Chapelle one day and visit the Musée d'Orsay and the top of the Arc de Triomphe the next, a pass will only cost you a few euros extra. One problem immediately picked up on by the Snob is that such passes encourage tourists to see as much as they can at breakneck speed.

This leads both to exhaustion and failing to savor the many splendors of the city. For Cheapos who have time to spare and prefer to save their energy by seeing only one monument per day, it's better to look elsewhere. Check the online site of the museum you want to visit and see what kind of price they are offering; the Louvre sometimes offers deals after 3:30 p.m. Better still, go to one of the FNAC bookstores [www.fnactickets.com] found all around town: at train stations like the Gare de Lyon, Gare de l'Est, and Gare Montparnasse, as well as on the main drag, the Champs-Élysées (8th), to give you just a few locations. These tickets only add a euro or two to the normal entrance fee but allow you to skip the long line, something greatly appreciated especially in the summer at the crowded museums. We felt a bit like royalty ourselves when we walked right up to the front of the line at the Pyramide and got in the Louvre in a few short minutes using this type of ticket.

Staying Connected: Wi-Fi

Wireless Internet is not available for free everywhere…make that, hardly anywhere. Some hotels charge a fee, but at American-owned businesses like Starbucks and McDonald's, for the price of something to drink or an order of fries, you will be able to connect at no additional cost. Public parks, too, usually have free wi-fi, but often understanding how to log-on requires at least a minimal knowledge of French and a maximum amount of patience. One note: a service in Paris called "Free Wi-Fi" is not free at all; don't waste your time trying to connect without having to pay for it.

Satisfying the Stomach

The Cheapo and Snob sides of you will not face any more serious struggles than seeking out the most authentic and tasty dining experiences without overtaxing their budget. Rule number one for peaceful coexistence: avoid any eatery on a major street, near an important monument, or having a Michelin star. The food is not always top-notch at such places and the prices will undoubtedly be high. For positive recommendations there are several French guidebooks which focus on deals for budget-conscious travelers. *Le Guide de Routard* and *Le Petit Futé* stand out in this regard and are now available in English. For a quick breakfast, try a croissant or *une tartine* (baguette with butter and jam) with a steaming cup of coffee, tea, or hot chocolate at a local café. Since eating out is always an added expense, you might prefer to get some *viennoiseries* (breakfast pastries) at one of the many *boulangeries/pâtisseries* (bakeries/pastry shops) which line just about every street. You can eat them sitting on a park bench or back in the room. For an even cheaper idea, drop in at the local supermarket (Monoprix, Franprix, Simply Market…) the night before and pick up something for breakfast: fruit and cheese or yogurt and bread, for example, especially if your room has a small refrigerator and you have the necessary utensils.

Likewise, a self-service lunch is another good way to save. Keep *boulangeries* or *supermarchés* in mind for a quick lunch or perhaps a picnic. What could be better on a warm, sunny day than eating your baguette with a bit of ham, cheese, or salami while sitting near the Seine or on the Champ de Mars in view of the Eiffel Tower? Another option is to keep an eye out for some of the thousands of *traiteurs*, a kind of deli which has prepared foods on hand. Asian shops of this type abound; you can usually eat-in (*manger sur place*) or take out (*à emporter*). Middle Eastern falafels can be found especially on Montmartre or the rue des Rosiers in the Marais (4th), and Greek gyros are found all over in the student quarter near the Sorbonne (5th). Of course, like everything in the food world, not all of these shops are created equal. After a while, though, you get pretty adept at judging the quality of the food by the look of it and sometimes by the crowds of people standing in line. A lot of small cafés in student and tourist areas have a window or display case which opens out on the street where you can buy some pretty decent sandwiches.

Having saved money with a do-it-yourself breakfast and lunch, it's time for a nice sit-down meal. In a city like Paris the options are plentiful from the smallest ethnic hole-in-the-wall to a four-star restaurant. But where do you go? Asking at the front desk might help in your search. Recommendations from friends you trust is another possibility, especially if they live in Paris or if they've been to the city recently. Guidebooks like the aforementioned *Guide du Routard* or *Petit Futé* or any of the other well-known books provide good advice. A favorite idea of ours is to find a neighborhood *bistrot*. Checking it out at lunchtime to see how crowded it is shows its popularity with locals. The chefs might not prepare the latest trends in food, but for a good, traditional French meal, this type of small dining establishment (also spelled *bistro*) is hard to beat. The food in such places is usually simple: *steak frites* (steak with French fries), *confit de canard* (made with leg of duck), or *cassoulet* (a white beans and meat dish which originated in southwestern France), by way of example. You probably won't get many green vegetables along with your dish at a bistrot, but the food is nearly always delicious and filling. Like in the U.S., having your big meal at lunch instead of at dinnertime is a real money-saver.

Searching for a good restaurant following suggestions in a guidebook offers a starting place. One tack that usually works out well is to look for recommendations in the form of small stickers (*étiquettes*) posted on the front door or window of restaurants or cafés as you walk through the town. These rectangular signs rate all types of fare and establishments. The size of a small index card, they might be issued from Cityvox, Trip Advisor, Le Petit Futé, Lebey, Gault-Millau, Pudlo, or Routard, to name but a few. Be sure to verify that the dates on the signs are recent to ensure a quality meal. Another possibility is to look online for restaurants before going out; you can search for the arrondissement you're interested in and also for your price range. Chowhound Paris usually describes the type of food in the various establishments and it's usually fairly easy to tell if it appeals to your tastes—plus English exchanges are frequently on this site. If you have some ability reading French, you can search *restos Paris* or something similar to find a world of information at your fingertips. *La Fourchette* (which also has The Fork site in English) offers a rating and reservation service with discounts for anyone who logs on. [http://www.thefork.com/city/paris/415144].

Satisfying Another Essential: *Les WC* [lay vay-say]

Restrooms in Paris pose a real challenge. Where to find one? This essential pursuit is not as simple as it might seem. Things haven't changed much since author H. L. Mencken visited the French capital in 1929 and offered this observation: "Cafés in Paris dangerously outnumber the *pissoirs* [urinals]." Places that we would consider a sure bet for having an available restroom—department stores, for example—hardly ever have facilities open to the public. Restaurants and cafés, sure, nearly always have a WC. You are usually in luck as well if you're in a mall or at the train station. Although there might be a restroom at these locations, however, it might cost you 50 centimes to use it; be prepared to have a single coin in that denomination in case there's only a machine on the door and no attendant. Here and there in Paris new installations are springing up which replace Mencken's old pissoirs which were intended for male users in past years. The current places are free, not gender-specific, and normally quite clean; the problem is you can't count on finding one when you need it since they seem to be clustered outside of the main tourist areas. You can always go to Macdo (McDonald's), though you probably have to make a purchase and might have to ask for a code in order to use the facilities. In a pinch, you could try searching the lobby of a four-star hotel to see if a restroom is to be had. By the way, ask for le WC or *les toilettes* and not *la salle de bains*—unless you plan on taking a bath! It's a good idea to have some tissues handy since, besides being stingy with toilets, Paris can be quite miserly with toilet paper as well.

Money Makes the World Go Around

Before taking off for France, you should talk to your credit card and/or debit card companies about several things. For one, you should make it clear that you'll be traveling abroad so that they won't cancel your card because of "suspicious activity"! Believe me, we've had this unfortunate and far from delightful experience. And number 2, you need to find out what kind of fees they charge for use abroad. And finally, you should ask them for the card's PIN which is sometimes required...like when you're buying tickets at a machine, for example. Another thing about those essential plastic cards, American versions (unlike the European ones) do not always have a chip and PIN—though national companies are definitely moving in that direction. For that reason, you won't be able to use cards without them in ticket machines at the train station or at tollbooths on the highway if you plan on any intercity driving. Better to be safe than sorry: have cash at the ready on the *autoroute* and go to the ticket windows at the station where cashiers know to swipe cards of this type in the other direction.

As a general rule, we have had good luck using our ATM card. One warning here, though, is that sometimes there are only numbers on the keypads, no letters. So if your PIN is a word, you will want to remember the numbers it refers to—just in case. Another thing to note is that there are often weekly limitations on the amount you can withdraw from the *guichets automatiques* (ATMs). Also, check the expiration date on your credit and debit cards. New cards arriving in the mail back home won't do you much good in Paris. So plan ahead, especially in the unlikely event that your hotel or restaurant doesn't accept credit cards. By the way, tips are included in France, so leave a few extra euros only for exceptional service.

Chapter 2

Free (and Nearly Free) Things to Do

AH, PARIS! THE CITY of Light, the City of Romance, the City of Fun. No big surprise here, there are scores of opportunities for entertainment, both expensive and inexpensive. Anyone wanting to find things to do in the evening should check in at one of the tourist offices at several train stations or the main one at 25, rue des Pyramides between the Louvre and the Opéra Garnier. You could also save some time and effort by doing your own research online at http://www. parisinfo.com/. Readers with a knowledge of French could go to one of the magazine kiosks to purchase a copy of *Pariscope*, a small, weekly publication that comes out on Wednesdays. There, you'll find lists of current plays, movies, concerts, and shows at famous nightclubs such as the Folies Bergère, Crazy Horse, or the Moulin Rouge. Although some of these outings might be considered low-cost, none are "no-cost." (And nightclubs would have to be put in the "high cost" bracket.) True Cheapos will be delighted to learn that other wonderfully free possibilities are there for the taking. Besides visiting the normal sights outlined in the following chapter, tourists—especially on a return trip or those wanting to avoid the hassle of seeing two big attractions in one day—might want to explore new parts of the city without spending a *centime* or very little! Some visitors may even prefer to have an atypical experience of the City of Light. Especially on a spectacularly beautiful day, strolling aimlessly through Paris—in all of its natural beauty, color, light, and architecture—is a sight in itself and shouldn't be missed. Create your own moveable feast, to paraphrase Hemingway. Take a walk. Have a seat. Relax. Savor as much as you can in one of the most beautiful cities in the world. Though you'll find many incredible splendors on your own, here are a few of my favorite promenades in Paris.

Along the Seine

For some lovely sights, take a long walk along the Left Bank of the river and check out a few of the various bridges. No need to visit all thirty-five of them unless that's the kind of thorough tourist you are. The beautifully ornate Pont Alexandre III, for example, which spans the Seine between the Grand Palais and Les Invalides, is a sight to behold and offers some great photo opportunities, including views of the Eiffel Tower. A short walk down the Quai d'Orsay towards Notre-Dame Cathedral brings you to a couple of interesting pedestrian bridges which are fun to explore. They even have some benches on them…just right for an afternoon picnic. Opposite the Musée d'Orsay, for example, you come to the Passerelle Léopold Sédar Senghor. You'll know you've made it there when you see a statue of one-time resident Thomas Jefferson to the left of its entrance. (See more about Jefferson in Chapter 8.) Continuing your stroll beside the river, you'll come to the Pont des Arts. This footbridge used to have padlocks left behind by lovers, an idea which spread to other bridges and locations on the Seine. (And even to the Brooklyn Bridge in New York!) But after a section of the walkway fell into the river in 2014, the government became aware of the danger of the weight of all of the locks and began removing them and putting up new solid sections. At the western tip of Île de la Cité, you'll find the simple structure called le Pont Neuf, the oldest bridge in Paris. Note the varied grimacing stone faces referred to by the architectural term *mascarons*. Then you might explore the nearby square devoted to

King Henri IV. You'll have no trouble finding the towering statue of the monarch on horseback. Wares of the *bouquinistes* (secondhand book sellers) line the river mostly on the Left Bank and are enjoyable to browse through for books, posters, and the like while you revel in spectacular views of landmarks such as the Louvre and Notre-Dame across the water. For about a month in the heart (and the heat) of the summer the annual Paris-Plages takes place along both banks of the Seine; here you can view sunbathers lounging on imported sand, pretending that they're soaking up the sun at the beach. Or, if you're game, you can even join in the fun.

Parks

Green spaces of all size and shape are to be found throughout the city. In fact, small "pocket parks" (or *espaces verts*) seem to pop up just about everywhere and offer nice surroundings for you to unwind or to eat a bite *al fresco*. Many wonderful large gardens—such as the Tuileries (1st), the Jardin des Plantes, and the Jardin du Luxembourg (5th and 6th respectively), as well as the Parc Monceau (8th)—are great places to relax, as well as to admire flower beds, fountains, statues, and that eternal favorite: people-watching. The Parc Montsouris (14th) and Parc des Buttes Chaumont (19th), while a bit removed from the center of town, are ideal for families and anyone wanting a break from the frenzied activity of traditional tourist locations.

The Jardin des Tuileries, named for the kilns which used to fashion tiles (*tuiles*) on this site during the 13th century, is centrally located between the Louvre and the place de la Concorde. After a day of sight-seeing and especially after a tiring trip to one of the world's largest museums, what could be better than to grab a chair near the Grand Bassin fountain, giving your aching feet a rest or planning your next move. A few cafés are found in this garden, but expect to pay top dollar, um, make that *euro* for this convenience. Near the northwest corner of the Tuileries, off the rue Saint-Honoré, you might like to pop by the former residence of writer Henry James at 29, rue Cambon (1st). If you're ready for a much longer walk, keep heading away from the Louvre toward place de la Concorde and eventually the Arc de Triomphe by way of the wide sidewalks of avenue des Champs-Élysées. Paris's main street, the Champs-Élysées is lined with cafés and expensive shops such as Hugo Boss and Louis Vuitton. Temptation surrounds the visitor in the form of all kinds of gifts and luxury items. Just past the Roosevelt métro stop on the left side as you make your way up the avenue to place Charles de Gaulle, you'll cross the rue de Marignan where a sign at number 10 indicates the long-time residence of American Impressionist artist Mary Cassatt. Farther up the Champs-Élysées, at number 92, this time on the right-hand side, you'll find another plaque indicating Thomas Jefferson's sojourn in the city when he served as Minister to France in the eighteenth century.

Discovering the Left Bank (la Rive Gauche)—Walks, Parks, and Gardens

The 5th and 6th arrondissements are home to Paris's university, la Sorbonne, as well as several delightful places to walk around. The Jardin des Plantes (5th), whose main entrance is at 57, rue Cuvier, offers a pleasant get-away from other more crowded sights in the capital. This botanical garden will charm you as it did many famous Americans of the past, authors Ralph Waldo Emerson, Henry Wadsworth Longfellow, Edith Wharton, and women's rights advocate Emma Willard among them. The spacious grounds of the Luxembourg Gardens near the Sorbonne (6th), one of my all-time favorite spots, can be accessed from several points including the boulevard Saint-Michel and the rue de Vaugirard. This lovely flower-filled park is well-equipped with chairs and benches where you can observe French families and their children playing, picnicking, or sailing small boats. If you like history, you're also in luck. The big building bordering the garden's north side that looks like a palace used to be just that. After the death of her husband, Henri IV (the guy on the horse we saw on the Pont Neuf), Queen Marie de Médicis had this residence built to look like the Pitti Palace in her native Florence. But, alas, times change—especially after the Revolution—and the building now has a more contemporary function as the home of French Senate. One of the miniature copies of Bartholdi's Statue of Liberty is located inside the Luxembourg Gardens on the western edge. A short walk away from there you could drop by 27, rue de Fleurus, long-time home to author Gertrude Stein and Alice B. Toklas and Stein's famous literary salon. Between the Senate and the Luxembourg Museum one also finds the temporary home of the novelist William Faulkner, the Hôtel Luxembourg Parc at 26, rue Servandoni, where he spent several months in 1925. Check out the white historical plaques at both addresses.

There are so many hidden tourist treasures on the Left Bank, including quite a few behind the Panthéon. A longtime favorite of ours is the place de la Contrescarpe (5th), a lovely square full of cafés between the Luxembourg Gardens and the Jardin des Plantes. Like one-time *habitué* Ernest Hemingway, you could spend an hour or more here, having lunch or sipping your beverage of choice and watching the world go by. Speaking of Hemingway, he and his first wife Hadley at one time lived a stone's throw away just to the north of the square at 74, rue du Cardinal Lemoine, which is also marked with a white plaque. A five minute walk away to the west of the Hemingway apartment house, you'll come across another free thing to do: the Arènes de Lutèce at 59, rue Monge. These ruins are old. We're talking really old here…like from the first and second century of Roman times when Paris was still called Lutèce. Off place de la Contrescarpe in the other direction toward the southwest, you'll find another blast from the Roman past which has fared quite well over the years. One of the oldest streets in Paris, the rue Mouffetard is also one of the liveliest. La Mouff', as the locals call it, gently descends the hill and contains all kinds of interesting restaurants and shops. A *marché*, or farmers' market, with all kinds of yummy things to eat takes place 8:00-1:00 every day except Monday at the square at bottom of the street.

In another part of the Left Bank near the Odéon subway stop close to the Seine, you can have more fun exploring two picturesque streets—the rue Saint-André-des-Arts and the rue de Buci (5th).

American visitors have been drawn to this area for decades. Poet E. E. Cummings once lived in an apartment at 46, rue Saint-André-des-Arts and writer Jack Kerouac, during his short five-day visit to the capital, hung out at a bar down the street at #28 now renamed Corcoran's Irish Pub. Close by, but over the administrative border in the 6th arrondissement is the small and very attractive square, the place de Furstenberg (6th) which is sometimes featured on posters you see for sale around town. This residential area was once home to French artist Eugène Delacroix and American mystery writer Chester Himes who lived around the corner at 3, rue Bourbon-le-Château at one time.

If you're up for a short bus or subway ride, you could go south to the 14th arrondissement to see the Parc Montsouris. Local families come here to enjoy the rolling paths, pretty lake, and pony rides for the kids and it's a delight for tourists as well. On the boulevard Jourdan, facing the park's south side, there is an international student residence, La Cité Internationale Universitaire, which has thirty-eight separate dorms housing students from different countries. A snack bar on the far side of the main building has refreshments and is open to the public. On the west side of the park, you could check out the area where singer-songwriter Nina Simone lived at the Villa du Parc Montsouris, 8-12 rue Émile-Deutsch-de-La-Meurthe. A few steps away, you'll find the hilly, curved street called Square de Montsouris, a unique and beautiful neighborhood, which has a house designed by renowned Swiss architect Le Corbusier at #51. About a ten-minute walk away at 101, rue de la Tombe-Issoire was twice home to writer Henry Miller in the attractive, cobblestone-paved, cul-de-sac called Villa Seurat.

Typical and Not-So-Typical-Tourist-Destinations on the Right Bank (la Rive Droite)

Okay, sure, Cheapos will want to keep a firm hold on their wallets on the Right Bank. Snobs, however, will be in seventh heaven on this side of town—especially if they're into shopping or at least hobnobbing at locations favored by celebrities. Temptations to buy are just about everywhere. Just ask Oprah Winfrey and Hollywood stars who spend their time in chichi shops along streets like rue Saint-Honoré, the Champs-Élysées; in Galeries Lafayette and Printemps department stores; and with designer fashions at Hermès, Prada, Louis Vuitton, and the like. By the way, if stylish clothing is your thing, and you don't mind the 70-euro fee, check the Hôtel Le Bristol website [http://www.lebristolparis.com/eng/news/fashion-saturdays/] to see if it's offering a "Fashion Saturday" while you're in town. The concept is for big design houses to present their current wares to potential customers who are enjoying high tea: a glass of champagne, finger sandwiches, pastry, and a choice of tea, of course. Imagine the bragging rights you'll have to impress your friends back home! The five-star (*oh là là!*) hotel is located at 112, rue du Faubourg Saint-Honoré (8th). It's probably worth dropping in just to have a look at the building itself!

For true Cheapos discount stores such as Monoprix or the huge Walmart-type retailer Carrefour are found nearly everywhere you look. Very small tourist boutiques scattered throughout the city offer the usual t-shirts, mugs, placemats and the like. Shopkeepers will probably reduce the price if you're purchasing several items so it's a good idea to ask for a discount (*une réduction*). Come on, be brave, give your French a try; it's worth the effort for a better deal, wouldn't you say? Neighborhood marchés, farmers' markets, have an array of fruits, vegetables, and meats and often have leather goods, linens, glassware, pottery, and other items for sale at reasonable prices. These markets are scattered everywhere throughout the city. For a combo farmers' market/flea market between Bastille and Nation at the place d'Aligre you'll find a Parisian favorite: the Marché d'Aligre (métro Ledru-Rollin, 12th). This outdoor market has food for sale along with booths containing flea market items. Don't miss the nearby covered Marché Beauvau which offers sights and smells to get your taste buds activated! Both markets are closed Mondays and vendors at Beauvau take a three-hour break in the afternoons on the days that they are open for business.

If you speak some French or are at least adept at using gestures, go bargain with sellers at the dedicated *marchés aux puces* (flea markets). Everything from knock-off brands and assorted cheap trinkets to crystal, linens, and treasured antiques can be found at several locations around the capital. From Saturday to Monday 9:00 to 6:00 the oldest and largest marché of this kind in the city, Saint-Ouen, spreads over a large area from the avenue de la Porte de Clignancourt to the rue des Rosiers in Montmartre just north of the boulevard Périphérique (18th). Back on the Left Bank south of the city on both weekend days you can shop at the flea market of the Porte de Vanves or on Sundays at the Arts and Crafts market on the boulevard Edgar Quinet (both in the 14th). Even if you're not buying, you'll have fun walking around, observing the locals, and looking at all the merchandise. Not in any way your typical American garage sale!

Besides the shopping opportunities on the Right Bank of the Seine, there are a few uncommon places worth your time. Cheapos will love these suggestions since (for the most part) they're absolutely free for the taking. Though, because of the distance between them, you'll probably want to opt for bus or métro tickets to get from one to the other. Starting out inside the Gare de Lyon train station (12th), you'll be surprised and delighted to find a beautifully decorated turn-of-the-20th century gastronomic restaurant, Le Train Bleu. Snobs might find the attraction too great and will want to stick around for a meal. Cheapos, on the other hand, could at least walk in to gawk at the *Belle Époque* beauty of this historical monument. About a five – or six-minute walk away up the rue de Lyon you'll find the Promenade plantée, also referred to as the Coulée verte (12th). The inspiration for New York City's High Line, it's an elevated walkway built on old railway tracks, making for a nice walk with pretty views and allowing you to discover an under-visited part of the city. A short subway ride away north to the 10th arrondissement is the Canal Saint-Martin, Napoleon Bonaparte's solution for getting water into the city. Lovely iron bridges over the waterway provide a scenic place to photograph, walk around, picnic, or just sit and watch the boats go by. About a twenty-minute walk west of the canal, you'll come to the rue Montorgueil (which straddles the 1st and 2nd arrondissements). On this charming street residents go out to eat, or shop for bread, chocolate, wine, and flowers. Don't miss drooling at the contents in the window of the oldest pastry shops in the city, La Pâtisserie Stohrer. Still going strong after nearly three centuries, the shop was founded by the creator of the famed rum-soaked cake: *baba au rhum*. You might even want to treat yourself to a pastry or two after the workout you've had!

Covered Passageways

Long before there were malls Parisians enjoyed running errands by way of a series of twenty arcades—mostly built to spare nineteenth-century shoppers from having to slog through the muddy streets of the capital. These sheltered passages might be considered off the beaten tourist track but they are without a doubt well worth the trip. Many are scattered about the Right Bank in the area of the Grands Boulevards métro stop. Not only do they provide a warm, dry place to be if you find yourself in the city on a rainy day, but they are architecturally beautiful with their glass ceilings, high archways, and mosaic floorings. You'll also have your pick of restaurants and be able to shop to your heart's content among the various businesses there. Five of them are located within a fifteen-minute walk of each other: the Passage Verdeau , 6 rue de la Grange-Batelière, the Passage des Panoramas at 11, boulevard Montmartre, the Passage Jouffroy at 10-12, boulevard Montmartre, the Galerie Vivienne, 4, rue des Petits-Champs, and the Passage Choiseul, 40, rue des Petits-Champs. If you become hooked on exploring these lovely gems from the past, most of the covered passageways are indicated on city maps.

Panoramas

Most visitors agree—Paris is the most beautiful city in the world. No exaggeration. So, it would be a real shame not to spend some of your time relishing all the beauty right before your eyes. Luckily for the Cheapos among us, free and low-cost vistas of the French capital can be enjoyed from many spots, quite a few of them on the Right Bank. In the 16th arrondissement, the palais du Chaillot (métro Trocadéro) offers the absolute best view of the Eiffel Tower looming in front of you on the other side of the Seine. Despite the inevitable mobs of tourists and vendors hoping to sell them all kinds of paraphernalia, you can't help being charmed by this impressive spot. After the obligatory photo ops, you might want to escape the hubbub: go down to your right where you'll find peaceful gardens in the Jardins du Trocadéro. Another Right Bank location, the steps of Sacré-Cœur basilica in Montmartre (18th), gives you a high perch to observe the city. Only the vigorous will want to climb the hill, however. Others should seriously consider giving their poor feet a break and take the *funiculaire* railway from the square Louise Michel for the amazingly low price of one métro ticket. The rooftop terraces of two department stores on the boulevard Haussmann (8th)—Galeries Lafayette (at number 40) and Printemps (at 64)—combine nice panoramas as well as cafés where you can sit and recharge your batteries. The glass-enclosed escalator to the top of the Centre Georges Pompidou (4th), the city's modern art museum, costs only a few euros and allows visitors a glimpse of many city monuments on a clear day.

Some will insist on going up the Eiffel Tower, natch. But for my time and pocketbook, three other perspectives are better suited to the Cheapo Snob lifestyle. Besides, as someone once pointed out, you can't see the Tower if you're on it! Now, take Napoleon's Arc de Triomphe on the Right Bank (8th), for example. Here you catch sight of the nearby Champs-Élysées, place de la Concorde, as well as the Eiffel Tower itself. The monolithic Tour Montparnasse (14th), a tower which novelist Saul Bellow once described as having mistakenly "strayed away from Chicago," is the tallest and, some suggest, the ugliest building in Paris. And while it might not be so lovely itself (there are plans to transform it), this tower offers magical sights especially at sunset when lights begin to come on all around the city. For the hearty and non-claustrophobic visitor, a third option is to climb the 350 or so narrow steps to the top of Notre-Dame. This prime location on Île de la Cité gives you a double pay-off: a wonderful view of Paris as well as a way to get up close and personal with the amusing waterspouts and statues, the gargoyles and chimeras, of the great medieval cathedral.

Churches

If places of worship, or for that matter, medieval buildings are your thing, you're in for a treat in this city. The "big two"—Notre Dame and Sainte-Chapelle (both located on Île de la Cité in the 4th)—are discussed in depth in Chapter 3. Like in most cities, Parisian churches (with the exception of Sainte-Chapelle) allow visitors free admittance. But one really nice thing in the French capital is that many also have free guided tours. Granted, most require understanding French but there are no-cost English tours of Notre-Dame on Wednesday, Thursday, and Friday at 2:00, and Monday, Tuesday, and Saturday at 2:30. (Check the schedule at www.notredamedeparis.fr to be sure the days and times haven't changed.) Look for groups gathered in pews toward the back of the cathedral—and don't be surprised if the tour starts a little late. Only we Americans, it seems, are slaves to the clock! If you read and understand spoken French, visit the site www.artculturefoi-paris.fr and go to the *Visite d'églises* section for information about guided tours at other lesser known locations around the city...like at Saint-Sulpice or Saint-Eustache, for example. Really worth your time.

Tours

Besides guided visits to Parisian churches, there are all kinds of tours to different parts of the city available, many in English. Of course, some are inordinately expensive—to the tune of 300 euros or more for food locations! Snobs will have to evaluate their worth on an individual basis. Not for Cheapos, that's for sure. Searching for "free English tours of Paris" online will unearth many sites. Other organizations, like the Paris Visitors' Bureau, for example, offer complimentary tours of a variety of landmarks as does a group called City Free Tours. These are usually very informative ways to get to know the city in a language we all understand, just the price of a tip for the guide. Convenient and cheapest of all, 100% cost-free guaranteed, you can create your own memorable expedition by using the addresses of the Main Attractions, famous Americans, and cafés listed in later chapters of this book.

Cemeteries

It may seem crazy to some readers, but graveyards are high on the free-things-to-do list in Paris. Artists, photographers, as well as ordinary tourists like you and me enjoy the park-like atmosphere and all of the stunning statues and bronzes adorning the graves. Parisian cemeteries really are, as a tour guide once told us, "outdoor museums." The sprawling Père-Lachaise, a bit out of the way in the 20th arrondissement, was named for the confessor of Louis XIV and has been around since the late eighteenth century; it's definitely worth the trip. You can get there by choosing one of three métro stops: Gambetta, Père-Lachaise, or Philippe Auguste. If you go in the main entrance on the boulevard Ménilmontant, you can get a guide map ("un plan") to find your way around. To save time, you might want to download the map from the Internet and chart out your itinerary before you go. An international group of famous people are buried here—from authors Balzac, Proust, and Oscar Wilde to singers Maria Callas and Edith Piaf. Readers might want to visit the final resting places of their favorite celebrated Americans, too: Isadora Duncan, Gertrude Stein, Richard Wright, and Jim Morrison—all covered in chapters of this guide. It might take you a while to navigate the curving and at times perplexing pathways of the cemetery. Morrison's grave has always been a challenge for us to find but I'm sure fans of The Doors will find a way to get there!

In the 14th near the Montparnasse tower is a cemetery of the same name. At the métro Raspail take the boulevard Edgar Quinet to the entrance and look over the posted cemetery map after you go in. Free, individual maps are no longer provided, it seems. But since it's much smaller than Père-Lachaise, it's much easier to get around. You should note, though, the cemetery is divided in two by the rue Émile Richard so the particular grave you're looking for might actually be on the other side of the street. Famous people interred here include

French authors Simone de Beauvoir and Jean-Paul Sartre as well as Americans such as photographer Man Ray, actress Jean Seberg, and writer Susan Sontag.

Museums

No, Cheapos, not all free things are created equal. You might have read, for example, that the Louvre is free on the first Sunday of the month from October to March. Yes, it's true. And while this may seem awfully attractive at first glance, even Cheapos might cringe once they see the interminably long lines at the entrance and then the crowds blocking your view and photo at every turn once you get inside. Better bite the bullet and pay to get in. If you want to see a museum at no cost, however, there are some other possibilities that won't test your patience to that degree. The lovely, always free Musée Carnavalet, dedicated to the history of Paris, is located in the Marais; it and the Louvre will be discussed in depth in the next chapter. Two other free museums which might pique your interest are the Petit Palais and the Musée Bourdelle. The Petit Palais on the Avenue Winston Churchill (8th) never was a palace, as its name seems to suggest. Created for the Universal Exhibition in 1900, it now houses the city's fine arts museum and its permanent collection is free to all. The building alone is worth the trip. A little farther afield the visitor will find the Musée Bourdelle, 16-18, rue Antoine Bourdelle (15th). The former studio of a well-known sculptor, a contemporary of Rodin, contains works and information about his art, including the friezes of the face of American dance pioneer Isadora Duncan which he created to decorate the exterior of the Théâtre des Champs-Élysées (8th). Very nice museums, both of them, which will appeal to most Snobs and Cheapos.

Cafés

Last but certainly not least, taking a seat at a small round table outside one of the hundreds of cafés offers relaxation, people-watching, and, it goes without saying, refreshment. Found on just about every street of the city, these celebrated Parisian establishments provide a not-to-miss experience for visitors. For the price of a cup of coffee or a glass of wine, you can literally occupy a chair for hours, and probably even most of the day if you're so inclined. No one will rush you; you won't be asked to order something else. Of course, cafés on busy streets (like the Champs-Élysées) or in high-class neighborhoods (such as the 16th) will most definitely come at a higher price. Probably the least expensive thing to order is, you might have guessed, wine. Definitely cheaper than beer or any other type of alcoholic or even non-alcoholic beverage. I kid you not, a coke or an Orangina will cost you more! And there's no need to order anything but a glass of the house wine: *un verre de rouge*, *blanc* or *rosé*. For dyed-in-the-wool Cheapos, standing at the bar instead of sitting at a table is always the least expensive, if not the most comfortable, way to relish an afternoon drink. Most cafés even have some kind of restricted menu and a *plat du jour* (a daily special) often posted on the chalkboard out front. So stick around for a meal if you happen to be hungry. Bon appétit! (See more on individual cafés in Chapter 12.)

Chapter 3

Main Attractions

AH, *LA BELLE VIE*–living the good life in Paris has been and continues to be a dream for many. And, as we have said, the French capital has no shortage of things to see and do. That's why designing your own travel plan in advance is always advisable…and can be part of the fun! If you have a mere three days or so for your visit, it's understandable that you'd want to see as much as you can as quickly possible. In that case it may be worth your while to buy some sort of museum pass which lets you skip the long lines at many monuments and museums. But, if time allows, the best way to savor the city is to visit one major attraction per day; two tops. That way, you can do a lot of strolling and lolling around, sitting at outdoor cafés, and soaking up what the city is all about. Any passes would not be cost-worthy for this stop-and-smell-the-roses type of travel.

To avoid bad surprises as you make plans, take into consideration which days the various venues are open; the Musée d'Orsay, for instance, is closed Mondays and the Louvre on Tuesdays. It's always a good idea, too, to double check days and hours which are subject to change. Lines can be quite long just about everywhere especially during school vacations and the summer months. A good site, jaime-attendre.com (ironically "I like to wait"—oh, those funny French!), estimates how long you'll be standing in line at the different attractions on different days and at different hours. Their use of a color scale from green (for short wait times) to red (for long ones) makes it fairly simple for anyone, even the critically language-impaired, to understand. Just make sure you know that *lundi, mardi, mercredi, jeudi, vendredi, samedi, dimanche* cover the days of the week from Monday to Sunday respectively and that *férié* stands for holiday; closed days are indicated in black on the site. So, here you go: my list of the top twelve must-see sites in and around Paris. *Bonne visite*!

La Tour Eiffel (5, avenue Anatole France, quai Branly, 7th, métro Bir-Hakeim)

On just about everyone's list of what to see in Paris: the Eiffel Tower. Iconic, revered symbol of Paris, right? Well, that hasn't always been the case. Far from it. Designed to serve as an entrance arch for the Exposition Universelle in 1889, the tallest edifice in the world at the time would soon become the object of intense ridicule. In fact, the barbaric "factory smokestack" prompted over three hundred artists and writers to compose and sign a letter of protest criticizing it for defacing the city skyline! Only its valuable function to transmit radio signals saved the tower from destruction when its lease expired twenty years later. How public opinion can change! Slowly, prominent figures and ordinary people alike joined its growing list of admirers. And what an architectural marvel it is! Imagine, a soaring 986-foot edifice, weighing in at 10,000 tons, but sitting as light as a 200-pound man on the ground below it. Thank you, Gustave Eiffel, for a job well done!

When it comes to really tall monuments, there are two kinds of people: those who insist on climbing to the top and those who merely want to observe it from the outside. For those "to the top or bust" people, fear not: the Eiffel Tower is open every day of the year. And visitors have several options to decide on. First of all, you'll have to pick and choose among the various prices and ways to ascend the tower—but all are quite reasonable. The very robust and cheapest of Cheapos might opt to walk up (and/or down) one or more levels. A compromise would be to take the elevator up to the desired level and walk down. However, this is recommended for healthy folks who don't experience vertigo while circling around in the descent, seeing the ground through the openings in the iron grillwork of the stairs! Take it from one who knows. Tip of the day: buy your tickets online and show up at the time indicated so that you won't have to spend hours waiting in line with hundreds of your new best friends.

Each level of the tower has its charms. On level one, you'll find several eating areas, a post office, and a gift shop as well as a film about the tower's creation. Going up to the next story there are several boutiques and a gourmet restaurant: the Jules Verne [https://en.parisinfo.com/paris-restaurant/70615/Le-Jules-Verne]. A *real* splurge for Snobs, this Michelin-starred eatery was Tom Cruise's choice for proposing to Katie Holmes…back in happier days. If imitating celebrities is your thing and, more importantly, if cost is no object, this might be just the place for you. Plan on spending the equivalent of at least one hundred dollars apiece for lunch and nearly three times that much for dinner—before you even think of what to drink! For what seems like a bargain in comparison, continue on to the very top, level 3. There, you can pay a more modest price at a champagne bar; you can also see wax figures of Eiffel welcoming Thomas Edison to his office in the tower, and check out a diorama of the monument's history. Of course, amazing views are to be had from any of the levels. Try to pick a clear day, though, since there is often a haze over the city limiting visibility and making it feel quite cool, especially at the top. For Romantics, try going just before sunset when you can see the lights illuminating the city and its monuments.

Not feeling the need to go up the Eiffel Tower? Seeing it up close is definitely a treat. Find a park bench and just sit, or relax with a picnic lunch on the Champ de Mars right behind the tower. Take your time soaking up the experience and admiring the lacy beauty of the tower's ironwork. Think about the 50 tons of paint needed to refresh France's Iron Lady, la Dame de fer, every seven years and the two and a half million rivets holding her together. Wondering about all the names engraved on the sides? They are to honor seventy-two top French scientists, engineers, and mathematicians. To get a great view of Eiffel's creation from across the Seine, make your way over the Pont de l'Alma to the place du Trocadéro and its gardens (16th). All of that beauty right before your eyes at absolutely no cost! I'd say that's a deal that's hard to beat.

From place de la Concorde, up the Champs-Élysées, to the l'Arc de Triomphe (Several métro stops will get you to this part of town: Concorde; Champs-Élysées-Clemenceau; Franklin Roosevelt; Charles de Gaulle-Étoile—all in the 8th)

Cheapos and Snobs will both have a field day in this section of Paris. To satisfy the Snobs, the eighth arrondissement is steeped in French history and filled with elegant stores. For the Cheapos, monuments and beautiful vistas are free for the taking. A good starting point on this journey is at the place de la Concorde at the easternmost end of the Champs-Élysées. While all is calm on the square these days, so-called "Harmony Place" was not always so peaceful. The infamous guillotine once stood here and took the lives of at least 1,000 French citizens, including King Louis XVI and his wife Marie Antoinette during the French Revolution. Thankfully, dodging traffic will probably be the biggest problem you'll face these days. So, just relax and enjoy the giant statues dedicated to eight major French cities, the fountains celebrating navigation on rivers and seas, and the oldest object in Paris, the Egyptian obelisk of Luxor. Impossible to miss, smack dab at the center of the octagonal space, the towering column was originally supposed to serve as the needle of a sundial. You're also standing right in the middle of the Axe historique—a perspective that leads your eyes from the Louvre to the pretty, pink Arc du Carrousel across the street, on to the obelisk at place de la Concorde, and the Arc de Triomphe. Modern day planners have added another landmark extending this perception of monuments all in a row: to the big square Grande Arche de la Défense business district west of the city.

For your next move, you could take public transportation or a cab to the Arc de Triomphe. Or, if your legs are up for a mile-long walk, find statues of the Marly horses marking the entrance to the Champs-Élysées and head up Paris's "Main Street." Shopping or just looking, the avenue definitely merits a trip. Elegant shops the likes of Cartier, Tiffany, and Louis Vuitton line the wide sidewalks and Snobs will find it hard to resist a purchase or two. Cheapos, on the other hand, will undoubtedly be aghast at the prices and will settle for window-shopping. (Three hundred euros for a key-chain, really?) Either way, it's fun to experience, if only to dream about how the other half lives. On the way up the avenue you might want to check out two plaques devoted to Americans: one to Impressionist painter Mary Cassatt, at 10 rue de Marignan, and the other to Founding Father Thomas Jefferson, at 92, avenue des Champs-Élysées. Both were long-time residents of the city and are covered in later chapters of this guide.

Napoleon Bonaparte, le Grand Napoléon, always dreamed big… while conquering foreign lands and designing monuments to celebrate his glorious exploits. After the pink-columned Arc du Carrousel across from the Louvre was completed, he set up plans for a second triumphal arch twice its size. The Arc de Triomphe commemorates the victories of the Grande Armée (and the emperor himself, of course). When you arrive at place Charles de Gaulle, though, it's hard to say if you'll be more impressed by the monumental arch or the impossibly crazy traffic swirling around it. (Lucky for tourists, underground passageways allow you to get there unscathed!) War symbolism naturally abounds on and around the arch. Snobs and Cheapos alike might want to take a look at the sculptures on the front. "The Departure of the Volunteers 1792" on the front right pillar symbolizes the Goddess of War rousing citizens to fight for freedom. On the left the Emperor Napoleon himself is being crowned with a laurel wreath by Victory as Fame sounds a trumpet above his head. Under the arch is the burial place of France's unknown soldier from World War I; its eternal flame, which inspired Jacqueline Kennedy for JFK's grave, is relit in a ceremony each night at 6:30 if you're interested. As with the Eiffel Tower, you may choose simply to observe the monument from below or you could take a trip to the top for panoramic views. Open daily except for New Year's Day, May 1st (French Labor Day), and Christmas Day for a reasonable price.

Notre-Dame (6, parvis Notre-Dame, place Jean-Paul II, 4th, métro Cité)

Napoleon was not the first Frenchman obsessed with creating colossal monuments in the French capital. Oh, no! Way back in the twelfth century, Paris bishop Maurice de Sully, decided he wanted a cathedral as grand as the one in the neighboring town of Saint-Denis. He then initiated what would become a two-hundred-year building project of Notre-Dame de Paris on the big island in the Seine, Île de la Cité. Like the Eiffel Tower which was called "barbaric" in its early days, a few centuries following the creation of medieval cathedrals, the term gothic—as in barbaric—began to be used to describe their style. Different eras, same idea. Author Victor Hugo is credited with helping the public fall in love with this style of architecture again by publishing his novel, *The Hunchback of Notre Dame*. Soon after the book came out, the French government allocated resources for architect Eugène Viollet-le-Duc to begin its refurbishing. Obviously a man with imagination and a sense of humor, Viollet-le-Duc couldn't resist his own additions: whimsical beasts called chimeras on the roof and a statue in his own likeness at the base of the cathedral's spire.

While standing in line with hundreds of others there are several things you can do to amuse yourself. To the left on the ground as you face the church there's a circular plaque which says "point zero"–used to measure distances to Paris from other French cities and towns. Legend has it that stepping on the marker assures the visitor of a return trip to the City of Light, so don't miss your chance here! Take a look at the architecture of the cathedral, too: the majestic double steeples, the line of statues representing biblical kings just below the lacy rose window, and the three large portals depicting the Virgin Mary, the Last Judgment, and Saint Anne. One humorous detail on the center portal: angels lead the saved into paradise as devils maliciously tip the scales in order to bring more sinners into hell. In the statues at door-level on the left you'll probably spot a figure holding his head in his arms. This is Saint Denis, an early bishop of Paris who was decapitated and then was said to have walked six miles north carrying his severed head.

Once inside the cathedral, the high arches of the center aisle (called the nave) will surely get your attention. Medieval thinking was that the church should uplift you like a prayer going up into heaven. If you search carefully on some of the large pillars, you may find the marks of the medieval craftsmen who created them. In the transept, the part of the church which crosses the main aisle, be sure to check out the beautiful stained-glass and rose windows. History buffs might recall the many important events that have taken place in Notre-Dame: the king's calling for the Third Crusade in the Middle Ages, Napoleon's self-coronation as emperor in 1804, and the religious service attended by Charles de Gaulle at the time of the liberation of Paris near the end of World War II in August 1944. Hearty souls who are not claustrophobic and don't mind climbing up a cramped staircase can go to the top of the cathedral for a small fee. Wonderful vistas of the city and close-up views of the celebrated gargoyle waterspouts and the chimeras will be your reward. While you're up there, you could see the 13-ton bell, Emmanuel, made famous by Quasimodo in Victor Hugo's novel about Notre Dame. As mentioned in Chapter 2, Cheapo Snobs, who want to learn about the cathedral's history, can join groups at the back of the church for a free English tour on certain days of the week. After the visit to the interior, reward yourself by visiting the small park behind the church. There, you can take a seat on a bench and admire the lacy beauty of the church's wall support system—flying buttresses. On a warm day, you may want to wander across the bridge behind Notre-Dame and have an ice cream cone at the famous Berthillon tea room at 31, rue Saint-Louis en Île (open 10:00-8:00 daily except Mondays and Tuesdays).

Le Louvre (99, rue de Rivoli, 1ˢᵗ, Metro Palais-Royal-Musée-du-Louvre)

Rome, as goes the adage, wasn't built in a day and neither was the Louvre. The enormous, sumptuous museum started out in 1202 as a modest fortress whose traces can still be seen in the basement. Then over several hundred years it was entirely transformed to serve as a residence for French royalty. When the monarchy became, shall we say, out of fashion during the French Revolution, King Louis XVI and his family were moved out of the palace and their royal holdings became a museum open to the public. As the collection grew, so did the space…and the crowds. So much so that in the twentieth century something had to be done to manage getting the people in and out of the world-famous museum in a more orderly way. Chinese-American architect I. M. Pei was chosen to fashion a new entrance, the modernistic Pyramide, quite controversial at its inauguration in 1989. Now, though, its practicality along with its beauty have caused the design to be generally considered a triumph.

There are not many bargains on getting a ticket to the Louvre. Cheapos might be tempted by the free admission on the first Sunday of the month from October to March. Better think twice. The museum attracts nearly six million visitors a year—and many of them seem to show up on those days! Suffering through enormously long lines and jostling to get views of the art works is hardly anyone's idea of fun, I'm guessing. But check the museum website for occasional price breaks. Maybe they'll reinstate half-price entrance rates in effect in the afternoon. Otherwise, on Friday nights the under-26-year-olds of all nationalities are admitted at no charge. For others, it's best to buy a ticket online or at a FNAC bookstore or you could get the Paris Museum Pass. A lesser known entrance is through the Richelieu Wing, across from the métro Palais Royal-Musée du Louvre. A sign states that the entrance is for groups and those with reservations only; not to worry, though, as long as you have a valid ticket. Once again, it's worth checking the site J'aime Attendre to find out the best time to visit in terms of crowds and long lines: http://www.jaimeattendre. com/musees-monuments/musee-louvre/affluence-musee-louvre. As a general rule, Monday mornings are optimal if you can get yourself up and over there that early! We never seem to manage.

How do you tackle over 400,000 works of art spread out over an area equivalent to eleven football fields? Well, in a word, you can't.

Not in a day or even a week and it's probably not a good idea to try. Some, who just want to be able to say they went to the Louvre, might like to take American humorist Art Buchwald's suggestion and spend a mere six minutes dashing through galleries to see the big three: the Mona Lisa, the Winged Victory of Samothrace, and the Venus de Milo! At any rate, think of this experience as an enormous buffet of art where it's better to pick and choose your must-sees in advance. Your strategy can be greatly aided either by taking a virtual tour beforehand on the Louvre website (http://www.louvre.fr/en/parcours) or by picking up a flyer of various highlights at the museum information desk. Snobs might not mind paying an additional fee for a 90-minute English tour—available most days at 11:15 a.m. and 2:00 p.m. Ticket, check; plan, check. So off you go. Just remember the building was a medieval fortress and a royal palace, so you might want to check out the medieval moat in the basement as well as other decorative ceilings, chimneys, and other extravagant touches as you walk through.

After the Louvre, you'll be more than ready to do a little relaxing. Trust me on this. Head west to admire Napoleon Bonaparte's first triumphal arch, the lovely pink-toned Arc du Carrousel, and continue straight ahead to the Jardin des Tuileries. Grab a seat, rest your weary legs, and enjoy the beauty of the surroundings.

Le Musée d'Orsay (5, quai Anatole France, 7th, métro Musée d'Orsay)

So you're in Paris and naturally want to see some Impressionist paintings. Well, administrators of le grand Louvre were never big fans of this style of art and only purchased a few works. To get your fill of Monet, Renoir, Cézanne, Van Gogh, and friends head to the Left Bank and what appears to be a train station. Which is exactly what it was. In fact, this beautiful Beaux-Arts building served as the model for New York's Grand Central. Like its relative in Manhattan, Orsay was almost destroyed when it could no longer accommodate modern trains. But instead of tearing it down, French president Georges

Pompidou came up with a brilliant idea: why not transform the Gare d'Orsay into a museum? There was plenty of art to be had for the late nineteenth early twentieth century time period; the Louvre, the Jeu de Paume, and the former National Museum of Modern Art all chipped in from their collections. And what a dazzling sight it is.

Lovers of the great Impressionist masters are in for a real treat: Monet's cathedrals, Renoir's Bal du Moulin de la Galette, and so many other beautiful and recognizable pieces. Finding Whistler's mother hanging among Impressionist paintings might be a shock for some, but all becomes crystal clear when you realize that the American artist was like an adopted son who spent many years living in Paris. (Check him out in Chapter 9 of this guidebook). But it's not only Impressionism that's represented here. Precursors to the movement like Courbet, Delacroix, Millet, and Ingres have some famous paintings hanging on these walls as well.

Compared to the Louvre, the number of works at Orsay is quite small. You could probably see the whole collection in one day, no problem. To get the most out of your visit, you may want to consider a one-and-a-half hour guided tour in English at an extra cost. The focus is on topics such as masterpieces of the collection or the nineteenth-century tour devoted to the Impressionists. Cheapos might be interested in the reduced entrance fee in effect from 4:30 to 6:00 p.m. or Thursday nights between 8:00 and 9:45. But just know that the amount of time is a little tight, especially since museum workers—who are eager to get home—start ushering you to the doors well ahead of closing time! Closed Mondays, the Musée d'Orsay is normally quite busy on Tuesdays because the Louvre is not open for business that day. According to the site J'aime Attendre, Wednesdays and Fridays are the best days to see what this jewel of a museum has to offer.

La Sainte-Chapelle (8, boulevard du Palais, 1st, métro Cité)

Speaking of jewels, this glittering chapel of stained-glass on Île de la Cité is not to be missed. While in the Holy Land on Crusade in the

Middle Ages, King Louis IX had paid, well, you might say a king's ransom for relics supposedly from the crucifixion of Jesus. He wanted to build a "Holy Chapel" worthy of these sacred artifacts, so he did it up right. He employed craftsmen to fashion slender pillars inside the nave and got stained-glass specialists from the newly finished Chartres Cathedral to create windows which recount Biblical tales. Look for laminated cards inside the chapel which describe all fifteen windows in great detail. In its 800 years of existence, as you can imagine, Sainte-Chapelle has been through a lot. Floods and fires, not to mention the French Revolution and two world wars. But it has survived mostly intact and what an inspiring place it is! Try to go on a sunny day to appreciate the full glory of its beautiful windows.

Security is tight at Sainte-Chapelle…mighty tight, since it's also the entrance to the Palais de Justice law courts. Expect to spend some time standing in line, followed by x-ray machines, and maybe even purse and backpack checks. Hours vary somewhat but in the summer it is open from 9:30 to 6:00, however no extra visitors are allowed in between 1:00 and 2:15. Once again, not surprisingly, J'aime Attendre says that the mornings, especially Tuesdays and Wednesdays, are best to avoid crowds. You can also buy a pass to get you into both Sainte-Chapelle and the Conciergerie, which can save you a few euros on the double admission fee. You'll have to decide if you really want to see the Conciergerie, the former prison which held among others Marie-Antoinette and Louis XVI. Personally, I would pass.

Le Château de Versailles (place d'Armes, Versailles)

Who would've guessed that a simple hunting lodge would one day become the magnificent palace at Versailles? It just took one man with grand ideas in the 1600s, King Louis XIV. To accomplish his vision for a new royal residence outside of the city limits of Paris, le Roi Soleil, France's "Sun King," spared no expense in design and materials. The final result: an outstanding creation which soon became the envy of other monarchs around the world. Louis—and a couple of royal descendants—lived a life of luxury here: entertaining themselves and their aristocratic friends with firework displays, the comedies of Molière, and lavish banquets. Even six-year-old Mozart dropped by to perform for Louis XV and his "official chief mistress" (believe it or not), Madame de Pompadour. Unfortunately, with all of the partying going on the kings and nobles failed to notice that the people were starving and were not so amused with the luxury at Versailles. The French Revolution, World War I, and the passage of time would take a toll on the Sun King's abode. But thanks to Standard Oil billionaire John D. Rockefeller, Jr. the château was refurbished in the 1920s and continues to be restored today.

If you think you might try to see all of the buildings and grounds at Versailles in a single day, think again. The seventeen-acre property is as overwhelming in size as it is in extravagance. A first-time tourist with a day to spend would probably want to stick to seeing the château and a portion of the gardens. Even this narrow a focus will prove to be quite a lot. Take your time enjoying the palace: from its stunning furnishings, murals, and gold-plated décor to its incredible ceilings and immense fireplaces. The recently refurbished Hall of Mirrors, or the Galerie des Glaces, was the famous site of the signing of the Treaty of Versailles in 1919 at the end of World War I. The baroque royal chapel has a marble floor and altar, white columns, and gold decorations. If you have the time, bring a picnic and enjoy sitting in the gardens, admiring the vistas, the fountains, unique statues, and the Grand Canal where Louis XIV liked to sail miniature ships and gondolas. Ah, to enjoy the good life of a seventeenth-century king!

To get to the city of Versailles, about 13 miles southwest of Paris, you have several options. For convenience and speed, Snobs might want to grab a taxi for about 50 euros. Cheapos, preferring the slower less expensive route, could hop a train from Gare Montparnasse or Gare Saint-Lazare. Better yet, take RER C5 and get off at the Rive Gauche ("Left Bank") station which brings you closer to the castle than the train. Once you get to the château, lines to purchase tickets can be long. And then the second queue to get in, especially on holidays and weekends, even longer. A wait of an hour or two isn't uncommon. For the best shot at avoiding throngs of people, buy your tickets in advance online and try to go from Wednesday through Friday early morning or mid-afternoon. The Château de Versailles is closed on Mondays.

Musée Rodin
(79, rue de Varenne, 7ᵗʰ, métro Varenne)

Auguste Rodin: brilliant sculptor or thief, scoundrel, and philanderer? All of the above, apparently. His life was, shall we say, tumultuous. The *wunderkind* often compared to Michelangelo began his studies by being refused admittance to the École des Beaux-Arts (Fine Arts School) three times. Despite the rocky start, however, he would go on to receive accolades for such well-known masterpieces as *The Thinker*, *The Kiss*, and the monument to Balzac. Rumors of cheating started in his mid-thirties when the statue of a naked man—L'Âge d'airain (*The Bronze Age*)—was so realistic that people suspected him of working from a mold of an actual person. But being that "there's no such thing as bad publicity," the piece put him in the public eye and soon led to fame and fortune. Another scandal followed when Rodin supposedly sold off sections of *Gates of Hell* before delivering the finished product to the French state which had commissioned the monumental piece. His tumultuous love affair with a young student, Camille Claudel, allowed him to borrow, well, let's call it steal, some of her sculptures...actually removing her name and putting his in its place! A complicated, disreputable man and a genius all the same.

Toward the end of his life Rodin moved into a beautiful eighteenth-century mansion, l'Hôtel Biron, now the setting for the Parisian museum devoted to his work. Located just off the boulevard des Invalides, the Musée Rodin has many of the artist's most famous pieces on display—as are a few works by Camille Claudel. Throughout the sprawling garden you'll find bronzes, such as *The Thinker*, *The Burghers of Calais*, and the infamous *Gates of Hell*. Snobs might opt to have a nice lunch in a café on the premises. Or for a couple of euros, Cheapos could just pay the entrance to the garden and enjoy their own picnic and Rodin's many sculptures on the grounds. An interesting "two-fer" is a combo one-day ticket for the Musée d'Orsay and the Musée

Rodin, which is feasible since neither museum is overly large. The Rodin Museum is closed on Tuesdays so Wednesdays are generally quite busy. The museum is free on the first Sunday of the month from October through March, but—once again, like the Louvre—it's undoubtedly packed with people that day and therefore not the best time if you're in the mood for a relaxing visit. Once again, for speedier entry, buy your ticket ahead of time online. While you're on the rue de Varenne, you might want to check out two of American novelist Edith Wharton's former addresses at numbers 53 and 58.

Monet's Home in Giverny (located about 45 miles northwest of Paris outside the village of Vernon)

Maybe admiring a few works by Claude Monet in a museum is enough for you. But then again, visiting the quintessential Impressionist artist's county home in Giverny is highly recommended if you're a big fan. Or even if visiting peaceful French villages is to your liking. Monet's connections to Upper Normandy go way back. Young Oscar, as he was called by his family, grew up nearby in the city of Le Havre and returned to the area after the death of his young wife. He spent time at his rural estate designing flower beds, building ponds and bridges, and, naturally, doing paintings of his exquisite property. Monet's house and garden have been totally restored and are open daily 9:30 to 6:00 from the end of March until November 1st. Spring is an especially pleasant time to see all of the different varieties of tulips in bloom. Whatever the season, though, try to schedule your visit for a sunny day to enjoy the multicolored flowers of the English garden in front of the house. The Japanese water garden, on the other side of the road, is full of asymmetry in the style of the Japanese prints Monet knew so well. The gardens and the house are truly a delight for the senses!

It takes a bit of time and effort to get to Giverny but you have several options. Renting a car for the journey to Normandy is a possibility Snobs might explore, but travel by train is, of course, cheaper and a nice way to travel. You can purchase tickets either online or at the Gare Saint-Lazare (8th) train station and reach the nearby town of

Vernon in under an hour. In the spring and summer there are shuttle buses that travel the short distance from the Vernon train station to Giverny for a nominal fee. Or if you're up for a walk, you could manage the five kilometers in about an hour. Another alternative for Snobs who can't be bothered with trains and shuttles is to take a coach ride from Paris [http://giverny.org/tour/] available from the end of March through October 31st…if you don't mind the cost.

Le Marais and la Place des Vosges (3rd and 4th, métro Hôtel de Ville, Saint-Paul, Rambuteau, or Chemin Vert)

Le Marais (The Swamp) hasn't been a marsh since the 1200s. Old habits die hard and its name hasn't changed over the centuries. Even after King Henri IV had a red-brick, royal residence created around the square called place des Vosges in 1605. Even after nobles started building stunning *hotels particuliers* (mansions) throughout the area. Always and forever le Marais. Around the time of the French Revolution at the end of the eighteenth century, once the aristocrats moved elsewhere, the chic area fell on hard times and was practically abandoned. Several centuries later Ashkenazi Jews from Eastern Europe revived the streets around the rue des Rosiers, developing it into a thriving commercial center. These days this same street is filled with food outlets selling delicious falafel sandwiches for a couple of euros. And the Marais itself has once again become a fashionable district of restored mansions, gourmet shops, trendy restaurants, fashion houses, museums, and art galleries. Perfect for Snobs!

Yet, Cheapos will feel far from neglected strolling through the Marais. Of all the free things to enjoy the aforementioned place des Vosges is a must-see. The oldest planned square in Paris, it offers a chance to sit in the park-like setting and simply admire the pleasing fountains and the red brick and white stone façades. Often live music of some kind is being played—by a harpist or classical music quartet—adding to the relaxing atmosphere. Another "freebie" on the square is the permanent collection at the Maison Victor Hugo, located at number 6. This home of the writer of *Les Misérables* and

The Hunchback of Notre-Dame is beautifully decorated and includes a Chinese-style living room designed by the author himself for his long-time mistress, actress Juliette Drouet. In addition, you will find all kinds of artifacts associated with Hugo and his family. The house is open daily from 10:00 to 6:00 except Mondays and holidays.

History buffs might like to have a look at another free museum, the Musée Carnavalet not far away at 16, rue des Francs-Bourgeois. Once the home of the Carnavalet family (and later of French woman of letters Madame de Sévigné), the museum covers the two-thousand-year-old past of Paris from its beginning as the ancient village of Lutèce to the present day. You'll find a bit of everything here from furniture and *objets d'art* to paintings and sculptures. Whether you are able to read the French signs in the museum or not, you will probably get more out of your visit by renting an audio-guide, available in several languages. The museum is usually open Tuesday through Sunday 10:00 to 6:00 and is closed on public holidays. It is currently under renovation, however, and won't reopen until the end of 2019.

Strolling around the Marais also gives you a rare glimpse of architecture from the Middle Ages. Baron Haussmann, city prefect on the orders of Napoleon III, did a pretty thorough job of wiping out what remained of medieval Paris in the nineteenth century. He did miss a spot here or there, most of which can be found in the Marais. Take a peek at the home of Nicolas Flamel, built in 1407, at 51, rue de Montmorency, off the rue du Temple. Other slightly more recent buildings can be found at 11 and 13 rue François-Miron, off the rue de Rivoli. Not a fan of medieval architecture? You'd prefer something more contemporary? The Doors' fans are in luck. Check out where lead singer Jim Morrison lived and died: 17-19, rue Beautrellis. (Read more about Morrison in Chapter 10.)

The Musée de Cluny and the Latin Quarter (6, rue Paul Painlevé, 5th, métro Saint-Michel or Cluny-La Sorbonne)

Ever wonder why a section of Paris is called the Latin Quarter? Do people actually speak Latin there? Well, they used to...in class anyway. Just like we saw with the name of le Marais, the Latin Quarter's origins began a long time ago and have stayed firmly in place. In this case Robert de Sorbon established a school for clergy in the 1200s, which came to be referred to as La Sorbonne. At the time Latin was the language required in classes. All these centuries later, you'd probably be hard pressed to find anyone who speaks a word of Latin around here, but remnants of the past remain. A great one is the mansion built by the abbot of Cluny as a residence for university students from his native Burgundy. A few hundred years after that, an archeologist made the manor his home and filled it with a variety of medieval art and artifacts. This collection became the starting point for France's "National Museum of the Middle Ages" or the Cluny Museum.

The building and its contents are an absolute treasure trove. Before going inside, take a look around the courtyard close to the entrance. You'll find carvings of snails and grapes which point to the Burgundian origins. Burgundy, after all, is well known for its escargots and wine. There are also shells of scallops ("Saint-Jacques" in French, James in English) symbolizing the pilgrimage to St. James Compostela in northern Spain which started around the same time. Once inside the museum you'll find a beautiful array of objets d'art as well as items relating to war and daily life in the Middle Ages. The masterpiece at Cluny is a series of six wool and silk Flemish tapestries called *La Dame* à *la Licorne*, The Lady with the Unicorn. In the *mille-fleurs* style, which describes the background of each covered with a thousand flowers, each hanging has, of course, a lady and a unicorn as well as a lion. The meaning of the tapestries is unclear but five of them are thought to represent the senses: the taste of sweets, the sound of a portable organ, the sight of one's reflection in a mirror, the scent of a wreath of flowers, and the touch of a unicorn. The sixth, À *mon seul désir* [To my only desire (or love)] may symbolize love, understanding, or virginity. At any rate, all are beautifully displayed in a specially designed room and well worth the trip. The Cluny Museum, open from 9:15-5:45, is closed Tuesdays.

For fun afterwards, spend some time wandering around the Latin Quarter. Just up the boulevard Saint-Michel in the direction of the Luxembourg Gardens, you'll find the lovely place de la Sorbonne, opposite the intersection with the rue de Vaugirard. If you take rue Cujas or rue Soufflot to the left off Saint-Michel, you'll arrive at the Panthéon, final resting place of authors Voltaire, Rousseau, Zola, Victor Hugo, and Alexandre Dumas along with scientist Marie Curie, among others. Just around the Panthéon to the left, you'll come upon the church Saint Étienne du Mont at the place Montagne Sainte Geneviève where Owen Wilson's character met the vintage car each night in Woody Allen's film, *Midnight in Paris*—now a popular tourist destination. A few steps farther down the rue Clovis, take rue Descartes to the right. At #39 you'll see the top floor where Hemingway rented a room to do his writing; nearby at 74, rue du Cardinal Lemoine there's a plaque indicating that the author lived here with his first wife Hadley from 1922 to 1923. (See more on the author in Chapter 5.) A few steps from the Hemingway apartment you'll come to the lovely place de la Contrescarpe, described in Chapter 2, where you might want to sit and soak up the atmosphere or have something to eat or drink.

Heading in the other direction, toward the Seine from the Cluny Museum, you will discover somewhat touristy but charming streets that are fun to explore. Going down the rue de la Harpe, wind your way through small medieval streets like the rue de la Huchette and rue Saint-Severin. You'll find all kinds of shops around, including restaurants and small eateries selling gyros and the like for grabbing a lunch on the go.

Montmartre (18th, métro line 2 Anvers, Pigalle, and Blanche stations and line 12 Abbesses, Lamarck-Caulaincourt, and Jules Joffrin)

Ah, Montmartre, a delightful hilltop area of quaint homes, interesting shops, and Sacré-Cœur Basilica. The area has always had its big fans but has also had a dark side. Once called the "village of sin," its reputation for wickedness started way back; we're talking the 3rd century here. The very name Montmartre—meaning "the mount of the martyr"—probably dates from the time Saint Denis, bishop of Paris, who was beheaded during a persecution of Christians. Montmartre had other brushes with naughtiness as the years went on. At one time considered a separate town outside the city limits of Paris, it wasn't subject to the same laws as the capital. All of the wine-making on la Butte (the Hill) led to wild partying and an influx of cabarets, brothels, and dance halls. Cheap rents in the nineteenth century made it appealing to artists such as Monet, Van Gogh, and Picasso, thus adding to Montmartre's bohemian reputation. Tawdry aspects continue to this day especially along the boulevard de Clichy where peep shows, sex shops, and cabarets proliferate.

But, make no mistake about it, there is a charming side to this section of the city which makes it well worth seeing. Its age-old architecture, like we saw in the Marais, wasn't destroyed during Baron Haussmann's revamping of Paris. So you get a village-type feel winding your way through the small streets. Probably the best wide-sweeping panorama of the city of Paris can be enjoyed from the steps in front of Sacré-Cœur. The wine-making begun during Roman times still continues at one vineyard on the rue Saint-Vincent. The winery called the Clos Montmartre continues to produce grapes and about 1500 bottles of not-very-good wine every year. Two windmills remain on the hill as well, including le Moulin de la Galette on the rue Lepic, celebrated in paintings by Van Gogh and Renoir. The nearby square, the place du Tertre, maintains the art presence on Montmartre, but contemporary Monets and Picassos are few and far between. In fact, you'll probably find more pickpockets and swindlers here than bona fide artists. The best way to get to the top of Montmartre is by taking a funicular ride, costing one métro/bus ticket; to find the cable railroad from the métro Anvers station, go up the rue Steinkerque, head left off place Saint-Pierre, go right up the rue Foyatier, and then left on the rue Gabrielle. It's about a ten-minute walk.

Intro to Americans in Paris

As Cheapo Snobs wandering around Paris, you are traveling in the footsteps of many prominent Americans. Why not take advantage and pay homage to some of our country's most well-known people? This activity is perfect for Cheapos (who usually need to invest the mere price of a bus or subway ticket) as well as for Snobs (who get to "rub elbows" with some of our national heroes). As a bonus, it's a great way to see and savor new parts of the City of Light. You know, "the other Paris"—the one normally hidden from typical tourists... neighborhoods where French people actually live, work, shop, and play. A good first step is to get a map. In Paris you could drop by a bookstore, like Gibert Jeune near the métro stop Saint-Michel (5ᵗʰ), and buy a copy of *Paris Par Arrondissement*. This handy booklet is available in hard – or soft-cover and contains maps of all the streets in the city arranged by district (arrondissement). Many editions have sprung up but my favorite is published by Coutarel—simple and to the point and only costing a couple of euros. You could also order a copy online from Amazon before you go abroad—but it costs about twice the price. Another idea is to search map websites on your mobile phone before hitting the streets in order to find your way around. Word to the wise, however: when searching for specific addresses, pay attention to streets with very similar names. It can be quite confusing and frustrating, for example, if you're looking for an address on the rue du Montparnasse while standing on the boulevard du Montparnasse; ditto with varying roads and squares called Clichy in Montmartre. Voice of experience speaking here! In the following pages you'll find short biographies and addresses of some celebrated fiction writers, journalists and other literary figures, politicians, artists and architects, musicians and performers, as well as a few other delightful yet unclassifiable personalities. To help narrow your search, the arrondissement of each location is given in parentheses. Some of the places you'll visit look just like they did in the past while others have completely changed. Still, exploring the city this way can provide you hours of interesting and practically cost-free entertainment.

An exhaustive inventory of every important American who ever lived in Paris is, well, absolutely hopeless. I've winnowed the list by concentrating on the most famous who have actually spent time living in the French capital…not just spending a few days touring. This means I have had to omit such big-name writers such as Nathaniel Hawthorne, J. D. Salinger, and Jack Kerouac. Another issue I faced is finding exact addresses for everyone. At times it was impossible to unearth the home address and I had to settle for the workplace location or favorite hang-out. Other times I found the street but not the number. Though an effort was made at accuracy, mistakes are easy to make; even people who were there, perhaps not too surprisingly, confuse street names, addresses, and even who was there with them. Anyway, have fun searching for traces of your American heroes; I'm sure you will. And you might even discover some new, fascinating people along the way.

Chapter 4

The Innocent Age (Fiction Writers from 1800 to 1914)

IT'S HARD TO PINPOINT exactly why, but for centuries now Paris has been a magnet for American writers. For some, it was the positive attraction of the city's beauty as well as its reputation as a vibrant intellectual center. Whatever the reason, way back in the early years of the nineteenth century, authors such as Ichabod Crane's creator Washington Irving, James Fenimore Cooper of *The Leatherstocking Tales*, and poet Henry Wadsworth Longfellow decided to settle for a time in the City of Light. As the 1800s progressed, children of privilege such as Henry James and Edith Wharton got their first taste of Paris while traveling with their families only to become residents later on. So here we have eight writers of fiction who, between the years 1805 and 1902, became the earliest group of authors to leave the U.S. seeking inspiration in Paris.

Willa Cather (1873-1947)

Raised on the Great Plains in Red Cloud, Nebraska, Cather would feature the small town and its people in novels such as *My Antonia* and *One of Ours*. At the University of Nebraska, the young woman studied medicine but developed a passion for writing after a paper she wrote for a class got published. Following graduation, Cather moved to Pittsburgh to work as an editor of a women's magazine. There, she met socialite Isabelle McClung who became her lifelong friend. In 1902 Cather made her first trip to Europe where she was "deeply moved" by the art culture. Her time spent in France especially felt like a kind of "homecoming." Because of her later trips to visit Isabelle and her husband in the French capital, Cather was no stranger to the city's often miserable weather. She nevertheless remained steadfast in her affection for Paris, which she described as "a hard place to leave even when it rains incessantly and one coughs continually from the dampness." Fiercely protective of her image and her privacy, she destroyed most of her personal correspondence, yet clearly had her closest relationships with women. In 1908 she met editor Edith Lewis, a Nebraska native, who remained her friend and traveling companion for the last four decades of the author's life.

Addresses for Cather

- 11, rue de Cluny (5th)—a pension near the Musée de Cluny where Cather stayed on her first trip to Paris in 1902.

- Hôtel du Quai Voltaire, still in business at 19, quai Voltaire (7th)—Cather and Edith had a room in this hotel around the corner from the apartment owned by Isabelle and her husband Jan Hambourg on the rue du Bac.

- 12, rue de l'Odéon (6th)—address of Sylvia Beach's famous bookstore Shakespeare and Company which Cather enjoyed visiting.

Samuel Clemens [Mark Twain] (1835-1910)

The often-termed "father of American literature" grew up swimming, fishing, and, true to form, pulling pranks in Hannibal, Missouri. A fictionalized account of the Mississippi River town eventually became the setting for his two most celebrated novels: *The Adventures of Tom Sawyer* and *The Adventures of Huckleberry Finn*. After a series of jobs as a young man, including riverboat captain, Sam moved with his brother to what is now the state of Nevada. Letters he submitted to the *Virginia City Territorial Enterprise* landed him a position as a newspaper reporter which launched his writing career. Using the pen name Mark Twain in the mid-1860s, he found fame with his story *The Celebrated Jumping Frog of Calaveras County*. Clemens and his wife Livy were frequent visitors to Paris in the late nineteenth century. Yet, he was seemingly unimpressed with the city, especially with its dismal weather: "…anywhere is better than Paris. Paris the cold, Paris the drizzly, Paris the rainy, Paris the damnable." Not a huge fan of Parisians either, Clemens described them as being chiefly concerned with "literature, art, medicine, and adultery." All in all, the French capital was a city he loved to hate and he undoubtedly relished the fodder it provided for his writing.

Addresses for Clemens

- Hôtel Normandy, still in operation at 7, rue de l'Échelle (1st)—Clemens and his wife found comfortable accommodations here on a 1878-1879 trip

- Hôtel Brighton at 218, rue de Rivoli (1st)—hotel near the Tuileries where the family stayed on a visit to Paris in May and June as well as early November 1894

- 169, rue de l'Université (7th)—address of the charming mansion where Livy loved to throw weekly dinner parties in the winter of 1894-95

James Fenimore Cooper (1789-1851)

Hard to imagine these days, but Cooperstown in Upstate New York was once considered a frontier village. Growing up in the town named for and founded by his father, young James loved roaming the "interminable woods" and listening to tales about the Iroquois. These experiences, coupled with his imagination, led him to pen such works as *The Last of the Mohicans*. Not strapped financially because of a sizable family inheritance besides marrying into money,

Cooper decided to abandon his Navy career and take up writing. More luck came his way when an appointment as consul to the French city of Lyons required practically nothing of him—not even the need to live there. So in 1826 he fulfilled a long-held desire and brought his wife and five children to Paris, their home base for the next eight years. Cooper's writings, well-known and admired in Europe, made him popular with such diverse folks as Scottish writer Sir Walter Scott and the Marquis de Lafayette. Although the city's perpetual gloom and muddy streets allowed for "a very great deal to condemn," Cooper enjoyed the views from the bridges and visits to the Louvre. In fact, he loved the museum so much that his friend, American inventor and painter, Samuel Morse portrayed Cooper, his wife, and daughter as figures in his monumental painting "Gallery of the Louvre."

Addresses for Cooper

- Hôtel de Montmorency, 10, rue Saint-Marc (2nd)—currently the Passage des Panorama, the family home for their first month in Paris in the summer of 1826.

- Hôtel Jumilhac, at 12, rue Saint-Maur (6th)—now the rue de l'Abbé-Grégoire, address of their third-floor apartment.

- 13, rue Saint-Florentin (1st)—where the family moved in December 1830.

- 22, rue d'Aguesseau (8th) and 59, rue Saint-Dominique (7th)— apartments the family lived in over the course of the 1830s.

Washington Irving (1783-1859)

The creator of classic tales about Ichabod Crane and Rip Van Winkle was first introduced to the beauty of Paris in 1805. A sickly young man in his native New York, Irving came to the French capital as part of a two-year European trip financed by his brothers in hopes of improving his health. What he found was at the very least distracting: a city full of "sensual pleasures," "the most fascinating" of all the places he visited. Irving led an active social life in Paris which included frequent trips to the theater and the opera. He spent time studying the French language and attending lectures on botany at the Jardin des Plantes. Irving was so busy, in fact, that he felt the need to excuse his short letters home by emphasizing that he was, after all, "a *young man* and in *Paris*." Following the death of his teenaged fiancée, Irving was inconsolable and spent long periods in Europe. After a while abroad, though, the worldly Irving became, he admitted, "a little callous to public sights" of the French capital. One bright spot came when, through his connection to the American minister to France, the author was informally presented to King Louis Philippe who expressed admiration for Irving's works.

Addresses for Irving

- Hôtel de Richelieu, 51, rue de la Loi (1st), now the Hôtel Louvre Richelieu on the rue de Richelieu, and then the Hôtel Jacob (rechristened the Hôtel d'Angleterre), 44, rue Jacob (6th)— Irving's first two accommodations in the city.

- Jardin des Plantes, 57, rue Cuvier (5th)—botanical garden and museum, the location of the lectures on botany he attended.

- 89, rue de Richelieu (2nd)—in 1824 Irving wrote letters home from this address which no longer exists

Henry James (1843-1916).

From his beginnings as the son of a prominent New York family, young Henry enjoyed a lifestyle which could hardly be described as Cheapo. Traveling extensively with his parents and four siblings, he first got to know the French capital as a child in the mid-1850s. Eventually, the young man attempted what he called the "Law School experiment" at Harvard, but his devotion to literature got the upper hand after he got his first story published. James then became a regular contributor to *Atlantic Monthly* and other journals. Seeking a "more active" place to live and write without the hard edge of New

York, he left for Paris at age thirty-two. To earn a living, James made arrangements to write bi-weekly letters for the *New York Tribune*. He initially loved the "glittering capital" where "charm, beguilement, diversion were stamped on everything." But, unable to enter into the literary circles of important writers such as Zola and Maupassant, he became disillusioned and moved on to London. There, he produced some of his most famous works including *Daisy Miller* and *Washington Square*. Although he never married, James had several female friends, including a deep, long-lasting affection for author Edith Wharton. A resident of England for forty years, James became a British citizen the year before his death.

Addresses for James

- 19, rue de la Boétie (8ᵗʰ)—location where the James family lived on trips to Paris in the mid-1850s
- Hôtel de France et de Lorraine, once located at 7, rue de Beaune (7ᵗʰ)—James stayed here on a short trip in 1872
- 29, rue de Luxembourg, now the rue Cambon (1ˢᵗ)—address of his Parisian apartment
- 58, rue de Varenne (7ᵗʰ) and 3, place des États-Unis (16ᵗʰ)—two apartments where Edith Wharton and her husband were living when James visited them in the French capital

Henry Wadsworth Longfellow (1807-1882)

Can you complete the line "Listen, my children, and you shall hear?" If so, then you are acquainted with Longfellow's poem "Paul Revere's Ride." You might be familiar with other verses about Hiawatha and Evangeline. Growing up in Portland, Maine, young Henry loved reading and studying foreign languages. While at nearby Bowdoin College, founded by his grandfather, he developed friendships with soon-to-be-famous classmates Nathaniel Hawthorne and future president Franklin Pierce. In 1826 Longfellow embarked on a three-year educational tour of Europe, arriving in the French capital in early summer. He and several other Americans took rooms in a boarding house where they had a curfew and were required to speak French at the risk of being fined. Longfellow was initially "delighted with Paris" and sights like the Louvre, Versailles, and Père Lachaise cemetery. He later complained that the city was "defaced with smoke and dust" and crisscrossed with narrow, muddy streets. Longfellow also grumbled about the French saying that they were not "overstocked with modesty." During his time in France, Longfellow spent ten days, mainly on foot, visiting the cities of Orléans and Tours as well as the châteaux of the Loire. He ultimately achieved great popularity back home and became the first American honored with a bust at Poet's Corner in London's Westminster Abbey.

Addresses for Longfellow

- 49, rue Monsieur-le-Prince (6th)—in 1826 Longfellow and other Americans stayed in Madame Potet's *pension de famille* at this address

- Le Procope, 13, rue de l'Ancienne Comédie (6th)—he enjoyed dropping by the oldest café in Paris

- 5, rue Racine (5th)—his second residence was an apartment in this building off the rue des Écoles

Harriet Beecher Stowe (1811-1896)

Abolitionist and author, Stowe was a well-known figure in nineteenth century America and Europe. Abraham Lincoln invited her to the White House where he allegedly said that her novel *Uncle Tom's Cabin* started the Civil War. As the child of a Calvinist preacher in Litchfield, Connecticut, she was educated as a schoolteacher before moving with her family to Cincinnati. There, she married Biblical scholar Calvin Stowe and began aiding runaway slaves via the Underground Railroad. While her husband was teaching at Bowdoin College in Maine, she came up with the idea of writing about the cruelty of slavery. Using a male pseudonym on articles in an anti-slavery journal, Stowe published weekly installments which were subsequently combined into her most famous work in 1852. The book's huge success—over 300,000 copies sold in one year—prompted the couple to take a break from the accompanying fame and controversy with a three-month tour of Europe. Stowe was delighted with the French capital, writing home: "at last I have come into a dreamland." On a second European trip three years later with her children and sister, the author stayed in an apartment near the Gare Saint-Lazare (8th) where she took French lessons and sat for a British sculptress Susan Durant.

Addresses for Stowe

- 53, rue de Verneuil (7th)—Stowe and her husband stayed at the home of abolitionist Maria Weston Chapman in June 1853

- 19, rue de Clichy (9th)—address of her second visit to Paris with her children and her sister—though they had to spend their first night elsewhere after they mistakenly were unable to rouse anyone next door at #17

- 65, rue d'Amsterdam (8th)—she and her family visited the home of French sculptor Baron Henri de Triqueti on several occasions

Edith Wharton (1862-1937)

A child of wealth and privilege, Edith Jones was well-versed in the practices of the New York upper class. But from the beginning she did things her way. No formal education for females? She schooled herself by reading books in her father's library. Proper women shouldn't become writers? She began composing a novel at age eleven and went on to become the first woman to win a Pulitzer Prize—for *The Age of Innocence* in 1920. She and her banker husband Teddy Wharton traveled extensively, but for the young woman Paris was a liberation on many levels. She enjoyed the stimulation of the city's intellectual community as well as the aesthetic beauty of the city's "architectural lines, the wonderful blurred winter lights, the long lines of lamps garlanding the quays." Sexual freedom came her way after her close friend, author Henry James, introduced her to an American reporter for the *London Times*, Morton Fullerton. Wharton's "ideal intellectual partner" then became her lover for several years. During this brief but passionate period they sent cryptic messages detailing where to meet such as "at one o'c in the shadow of" a particular painting at the Louvre. Her extensive charitable efforts during World War I led to Wharton being awarded France's Légion d'honneur.

Addresses for Wharton

- 61, avenue Josephine (18th)—as a child, Edith Jones and her family spent two years at this Right Bank address

- 53 and 58, rue de Varenne (7th)—she and her husband rented the apartment of George Vanderbilt at #58 near the Rodin Museum in 1906; four years later Edith left Teddy Wharton and moved to #53 down the street; notice the plaque dedicated to Wharton at #58

- 3, place des États-Unis (16th)—in the spring of 1908 Wharton stayed in her brother Harry's townhouse; a white historical plaque marks this building as well

- 25, rue de l'Université—site of Wharton's first workroom where she employed women to make clothes for refugees during World War I

- Hôtel de Crillon, 10, place de la Concorde (8th)—luxurious hotel, still in operation, where Wharton took a room whenever she needed temporary housing

- Cimetière des Gonards, 19, rue de la Porte du Buc—cemetery not far from the Château of Versailles where Wharton is buried

Chapter 5

The Lost Generation (Fiction Writers from World War I to 1929)

THE BIGGEST EXPLOSION OF poets, novelists, and playwrights to head for the City of Light occurred during the years following World War I. In fact, by the early 1920s the number of Americans in Paris—famous and otherwise—increased from about 6,000 to over 30,000! Several writers had gotten their first taste of the city while serving as ambulance drivers during the Great War: E. E. Cummings, John Dos Passos, and Ernest Hemingway among them. Most were termed "the Lost Generation" by Gertrude Stein who observed the disillusionment following the horrors of the First World War and the subsequent change in American values. What follows in this chapter is an alphabetical list of 21 fiction writers, from Sherwood Anderson to William Carlos Williams, who spent time living in the French capital during those tumultuous years.

Sherwood Anderson (1876-1941)

Hardly a household name these days, Anderson was once a highly respected author. So much so that he served as an adviser to Faulkner and Hemingway and an inspiration to future writers such as Norman Mailer, John Steinbeck, and Thomas Wolfe. A restless type, the Ohio-born Anderson didn't stick with one thing very long, be it cities, jobs, or even wives. After his short story collection *Winesburg, Ohio* secured his reputation in 1919, he and wife #2 traveled to Paris. Like so many American expats, Anderson was greatly impressed with the city: "I have never thought anything on earth could be so beautiful." Passing by Shakespeare and Company, he noticed a copy of his book in the window and presented himself to Sylvia Beach. The bookstore owner provided him with a letter of introduction to meet with Gertrude Stein at her apartment on the rue de Fleurus. Anderson also came in contact with other members of the English-speaking Parisian literary scene such as Ezra Pound and James Joyce. On a subsequent trip, Anderson got reacquainted with Ernest Hemingway who, ever jealous of successful authors, soon ended the friendship. An unfaithful husband, like Hemingway, Anderson nevertheless remained with wife #4 for the last eight years of his life.

Addresses for Anderson

- Hôtel d'Angleterre, 44, rue Jacob (6th)—then called the Hôtel Jacob, the site of Anderson's first sojourn in Paris

- Hôtel Regnard, 4, rue Regnard (6th)—former hotel near the Luxembourg Gardens where the author stayed on his second trip

- Brasserie Lipp at 151, boulevard Saint-Germain (6th)—popular restaurant which he enjoyed a short walk away from his hotel

- 27, rue de Fleurus (6th)—Gertrude Stein's apartment and site of her literary salon

- 20, rue Jacob (6th)—Natalie Barney's home and literary salon [See entries for Stein and Barney later on in this chapter]

Djuna Barnes (1892-1982)

From her unconventional family life in Storm King Mountain, New York, Barnes went on to become a central literary figure in post-World War I Paris. Described by one critic as a "carnival barker," the young woman was never shy about her skills as a writer and illustrator. At age twenty she walked into the newspaper offices of the *Brooklyn Daily Eagle* and declared: "I can draw. I can write. You'd be foolish not to hire me." Sent by *McCall's* to produce magazine articles from the French capital, Barnes was initially unimpressed with the city but came to regard it as one of her favorite places. She befriended other authors including Gertrude Stein and Janet Flanner and was a favored guest at Natalie Barney's literary salon. Having wealthy patrons such as Barney and Peggy Guggenheim enabled Barnes to remain in Paris for nearly two decades. For eight of those years she lived with American sculptor Thelma Wood, a relationship which served as the basis for Barnes's famous semi-autobiographical novel, *Nightwood*. Before her death in Greenwich Village at age ninety, Barnes penned a memoir with the revealing title *Life Is Painful, Nasty, and Short...In My Case It Has Only Been Painful and Nasty.*

Addresses for Barnes

- 20, rue Jacob (6ᵗʰ)—Natalie Barney's home and literary salon where Barnes was a frequent guest

- 173, boulevard Saint-Germain (7ᵗʰ)—Barnes and Wood first had an apartment at this address, now the flagship store of Ralph Lauren

- 9, rue Saint-Romain (6ᵗʰ)—the couple took an apartment in this red brick building in 1927

Natalie Clifford Barney (1876-1972)

The complete opposite of a Cheapo, Barney, while only in her twenties, inherited millions from industrialist father. She was then able to live the high life in Paris and to support writers she met at her literary salon. Her love of all things French led to leaving her hometown of Dayton, Ohio for the City of Light at age twenty-two with her first love, Eva Palmer. During a later relationship with a female poet, Barney tried her hand at writing and got some poems published. Her father, not amused with the lesbian themes, bought up the publisher's stock and had all of the printing plates destroyed. Barney's literary salon began at her home in suburban Neuilly and continued after she moved to the Left Bank. For over six decades her Friday night gathering on the rue Jacob attracted international and American artists and writers such as Djuna Barnes, Janet Flanner, Isadora Duncan, and Truman Capote. To promote the work of female authors Barney founded a counterpart to the Académie Française appropriately called the Académie des Femmes (Women's Academy). Non-monogamous by choice, she nevertheless maintained a relationship with American painter Romaine Brooks for over fifty years. Barney, who never returned to live in the U.S., is buried in the cemetery at Passy.

Addresses for Barney

- 4, rue Chalgrin (16th)—where Barney lived with Eva Palmer near the Arc de Triomphe

- 20, rue Jacob (6th)—her home and site of the famous literary salon she hosted for over sixty years

- 2, rue du Commandant Schloesing (16th)—Barney's burial place at a cemetery in Passy near Trocadéro

Kay Boyle (1902-1992)

"The other writer from Saint Paul," as she was called, was once as well known for her works as Scott Fitzgerald. Oh, but how times and tastes change; today Boyle's books go largely unread. Working as a young writer and editor in New York, she married French exchange student Richard Brault and moved with him to France in 1923. Boyle separated from her husband a few years later and began a love affair with magazine editor Ernest Walsh. Following Walsh's premature death, she earned a living as a ghostwriter in Paris for British aristocrat Gladys Palmer Brooke. Boyle loved the French capital and saw her arrival there "as a pilgrimage," most likely for the inspiration it provided authors of the time. With friends from artistic and literary circles, she patronized the grand cafés of Saint-Germain and Montparnasse. Yet, Boyle was unimpressed with Ernest Hemingway, whom she described as "unspeakable." The ever-critical Gertrude Stein had once invited the younger woman to her apartment on the rue de Fleurus but, finding her as "incurably middle-class" as Hemingway, never asked her back. Despite a turbulent life of sex, alcohol, and drugs in her youth, Boyle managed to live to be ninety years old.

Addresses for Boyle

- 17, rue Louis-David (16th)—Boyle lived at this address while working on Brooke's memoirs

- 27, rue de Fleurus (6th)—site of Stein's apartment near the Jardin du Luxembourg

- Brasserie Lipp 151, boulevard Saint-Germain (6th), La Coupole 102, boulevard du Montparnasse (14th), Le Select 99, boulevard du Montparnasse (6th), and Café de la Paix 5, place de l'Opéra (9th)—as well as the now defunct Bricktop's cabaret place Pigalle in Montmartre (9th)—some of Boyle's favorite hangouts

- Hôtel de France et Choiseul, (now the Hôtel Costes), 239, rue Saint-Honoré (1st)—a one-time home for Boyle, husband #3 Laurence Vail, and her six children

Hart Crane (1899-1932)

The very epitome of the Lost Generation, Hart Crane led a tempestuous life. So much so in fact that a friend once described him as more like a hurricane than a man. Yet, in spite of his unbridled behavior, he produced two influential volumes of poetry, including *The Bridge* in 1930. Leaving high school in Ohio before graduation, Crane moved to New York where he got to know authors Eugene O'Neill, John Dos Passos, and E. E. Cummings. Jealous of friends traveling in Europe, he left for Paris with letters of introduction to Gertrude Stein and French novelist André Gide. Crane associated with other expats in the city including Kay Boyle and Glenway Wescott. After meeting banking heir Harry Crosby and his wife, Crane began spending time at their home on the Left Bank and writing at their retreat in suburban Ermenonville.

While sometimes disappointed in Paris, he claimed that it was "the most interesting madhouse in the world," perhaps just the place for a wild man like him. Infamous for his drunken rampages, Crane once fought with waiters about his tab at a café in Montparnasse and ended up spending a week in a Parisian jail. Tragically, he jumped to his death from the deck of a steamship in the Gulf of Mexico at age thirty-two.

Addresses for Crane

- Hôtel Jacob (currently the Hôtel d'Angleterre), 44, rue Jacob (6th)—Crane's first lodging in Paris

- Les Deux Magots 6, place Saint-Germain (6th)—where Crane first met Harry Crosby

- 19, rue de Lille (7th)—home of friends Harry and Caresse Crosby which Crane often visited

- Villa Seurat 101, rue de la Tombe Issoire (14th)—the poet lived for a while at artist Eugene McCown's apartment

- Le Select 99, boulevard du Montparnasse (14th)—site of the fight with waiters which landed Crane in jail

- Prison de la Santé 42, rue de la Santé (14th)—where Crane was incarcerated for a week after his drunken brawl at Le Select

E. E. (Edward Estlin) Cummings (1894-1962)

Child prodigy turned Renaissance man, Cummings was a poet, artist, essayist, and playwright. Ironically, though, he is probably best known by most Americans for his lack of capital letters and punctuation. Like other authors of his era, the Cambridge, Massachusetts native made his first trip to Paris as part of an ambulance corps during World War I. Through an administrative error, Cummings and his friend—future writer William Slater Brown—failed to receive their assignments. Which brings us to another paradox: instead of dangerous work picking up injured soldiers at the Front, the two men enjoyed five weeks living the good life wandering around the capital. They went to the ballet and the Louvre, shopped for books at the bouquinistes along the Seine, and enjoyed relaxing at cafés. After the conflict Cummings returned to Paris, a city he termed a "divine section of eternity." Besides writing, he loved sketching various scenes—women buying groceries at the marché and children laughing at puppet shows in the park. Cummings also socialized with fellow expatriate authors such as Ezra Pound and Archie MacLeish. In 1933 he and his wife returned for an extended stay in the French capital aided by a Guggenheim fellowship.

Addresses for Cummings

- 7, rue François 1er (8th)—previous headquarters for the Norton-Harjes ambulance corps
- Hôtel Marignan, 13, rue du Sommerard (5th)—Cummings and William Slater Brown shared a room at this address in 1921
- La Reine Blanche, 79, boulevard Saint-Germain (6th)—the author preferred to do his writing at this former café instead of the larger more popular places along the boulevard Montparnasse
- 46, rue Saint-André-des-Arts (6th)—Cummings rented a single room here in 1923
- 10, rue de Douanier, now the rue Georges-Braque (14th)—the apartment at this address was "a palace" for Cummings and his wife in 1933
- 11, rue de la Bûcherie (5th)—a more modest studio the couple rented on a subsequent visit

Hilda Doolittle (1886-1961)

Growing up in Bethlehem, Pennsylvania, "H. D." had friends like Ezra Pound, Marianne Moore, and William Carlos Williams. How lucky to hang out with upcoming poets when you're gearing up for that kind of future yourself. In 1911 she left Bryn Mawr because of grades and health issues and traveled to Paris with her love, Frances Gregg. On a return trip the following year, Doolittle toured the city with Pound and novelist Richard Aldington. At around the same time Pound, her one-time fiancé, submitted some of Doolittle's poems to *Poetry* magazine, which began her literary career. After marrying Aldington and having a daughter with composer Cecil Gray, H. D. became the lifelong partner of the heiress/novelist Annie Winifred Ellerman, known as Bryher. A fragile person who struggled with her bisexuality, Doolittle became a patient of Freud in Vienna for a while in the 1930s. She also found comfort in going to museums like the Louvre which she felt could "hold one together, keep one from going to bits." In Paris, Bryher and H.D. were close to other expats like Gertrude Stein and Sylvia Beach, but never felt truly at home in the city. Once settled in Switzerland, they occasionally returned to the French capital, visiting friends, enjoying restaurants as well as Bricktop's nightclub in Montmartre.

Addresses for Doolittle

- 92, rue Raynouard (16th)— German pianist Walter Rummel gave concerts at his home which Doolittle attended in 1911

- 21, rue Jacob, (6th)—a pension where she lived for a short time

- Hôtel Continental (now the Westin Paris), 3, rue de Castiglione (1st) or Hôtel Unic, still in operation at 56, rue du Montparnasse (14th)—hotels Doolittle and Bryher favored on visits from their home in Switzerland

- L'Avenue, 41, avenue Montaigne (8th)—a Right Bank restaurant preferred by H.D.—and even today by contemporary American celebrities

John Dos Passos (1896-1970)

Called "the greatest writer of our time" by Jean-Paul Sartre, Dos Passos was also one of his generation's most nomadic people. He came by the travel bug early as a result of his "hotel childhood" touring European capitals with his mother. During the First World War, the Chicago native served as a volunteer ambulance driver in France and Italy with his Harvard classmate E. E. Cummings. Following the conflict, "Dos" returned to Paris to study at the Sorbonne and to work on novels such as *Three Soldiers*. After an itinerant period in the early 1920s, Dos Passos was back in the French capital, frequenting the famous cafés of Montparnasse with Ernest Hemingway. Try as he might, Hemingway was unable to communicate his passion for bicycle races at the one-time Vélodrome d'hiver and horse races at Longchamps in the Bois de Boulogne to his friend. Dos Passos was much more interested in their picnics of wine, cheese, and pâté than the competitions at the Vélodrome which he said had "a special comical air." After publishing his celebrated *U.S.A.* trilogy in the 1930s, Dos Passos served as a magazine journalist and war correspondent in Paris during World War II.

Addresses for Dos Passos

- 7, rue François 1er (8th)—former site of the Norton-Harjes Ambulance Corps

- Rendez-vous des Mariniers, previously at 33, quai d'Anjou (4th)—Dos Passos rented an upstairs room at this one-time hotel/bistro where the owner, Madame Lecomte, recalled darning his socks

- 45, quai de la Tournelle (5th)—Dos Passos took over the apartment of playwright John Howard Lawson at this address for two years

- Salle Gaveau, 45-47, rue de la Boétie (8th)—concert hall where he met fellow music-lover Germaine Lucas-Championnière whom he courted at her mother's home at 52, rue de Clichy (9th)

- Hôtel Scribe, 1, rue Scribe (9th)—luxury hotel where Dos Passos stayed when he was a war correspondent during World War II

T. S. (Thomas Stearns) Eliot (1888-1965)

Tom Eliot began his journey toward becoming the "philosopher poet" as a youth in Saint Louis. When physical problems limited his outdoor activity, the boy turned to reading and writing poetry.

He earned an undergraduate degree in philosophy at Harvard and in 1910 decided to spend a postgraduate year at the Sorbonne. In his essay, "What France Means to You," Eliot described his "exceptional good fortune" of living in the French capital, then the intellectual and cultural center of the world. There were friends to meet, like bookstore owners Sylvia Beach and Adrienne Monnier, cafés to frequent, and, of course, exceptional sights to see. Too much of all of the above perhaps. For the main danger, as he saw it, was that Paris is "a strong stimulant and like most stimulants incites to rushing about and produces a pleasant illusion of great mental activity rather than the solid results of hard work." Later, while working in London, Eliot decided to try to make a living writing. With the help of friend Ezra Pound he got his poem "The Love Song of J. Alfred Prufrock" published in *Poetry* magazine, launching his career. Eliot, who received the Nobel Prize for Literature in 1948, went on to become a British citizen and never returned to his home country.

Addresses for Eliot

- Hôtel Lenox, 9, rue de l'Université (7th)—formerly a pension where the author first stayed in Paris

- 151 bis, rue Saint-Jacques (5th)— address of the Cazaubon family who rented a room in their pension to Eliot

- Collège de France, rue des Écoles (5th)—university that sponsored lectures by Henri Bergson which the young man attended

- La Rotonde at 105, boulevard du Montparnasse (6th)—one of the grand cafés of Montparnasse that Eliot patronized

William Faulkner (1897-1962)

The winner of the Nobel Prize for Literature in 1949 never thought much of his writing when he was young. Yet, thanks to the encouragement of fellow author Sherwood Anderson, Faulkner was able to get his novel, *Soldiers' Pay,* published by age thirty. At around the same time the Mississippi native took off for what he believed would be several years in Europe. Things didn't work out as he had planned, however. Painfully shy, Bill never really connected with other members of the Lost Generation in Paris. He had letters of introduction to meet Ezra Pound and T. S. Eliot but never used them. He visited Gertrude Stein's literary salon only a couple of times even though her apartment was just a short walk away from his rooming house. Faulkner noticed Irish author James Joyce in a local café but didn't have the courage to approach him. As he wrote to his mother, unlike other expat writers, he had "failed to get the café habit." Instead, he preferred spending time in the nearby Luxembourg Gardens which he eventually described in the final scene of his novel, *Sanctuary*. Missing home and apparently uninspired in Europe, he returned to the U.S. after a mere 129 days abroad.

Addresses for Faulkner

- Hôtel Luxembourg Parc at 26, rue Servandoni (6th)—the once run-down rooming house, now a chic hotel, across from the Luxembourg Gardens has a white historical plaque which indicates Faulkner's stay

- 27, rue de Fleurus (6th)—address of Stein's apartment and literary salon which the author visited a few times

- Café de l'Odéon, place de l'Odéon (6th)—Faulkner noticed James Joyce at this café but was too shy to speak to him

- Shakespeare and Company 12, rue de l'Odéon (6th)—famous bookstore that Faulkner visited without introducing himself to the owner, Sylvia Beach

F. Scott Fitzgerald (1896-1940)

Handsome, bright, and ambitious, Francis Scott Key Fitzgerald was a relative of the lyricist of "The Star-Spangled Banner." He left his hometown of St. Paul, Minnesota for college at Princeton but dropped out after being placed on academic probation. Fitzgerald then joined army officer training school and was assigned to Montgomery,

Alabama. There, he met Zelda Sayre who agreed to marry him after his novel, *This Side of Paradise,* was published in 1920. To support their lavish lifestyle, he began publishing short stories in magazines like the *Saturday Evening Post.* Fitzgerald sought a resolution to marital problems by moving with his wife and young daughter Scottie to Valescure on the French Riviera. Believing that "the best of America drifts to Paris," Fitzgerald and his family visited the city frequently over an eight-year period, often for months at a time. He and Zelda stayed at the Hôtel Ritz where they became closely acquainted with its luxurious bar. In fact, Fitzgerald's Parisian life pretty much revolved around cafés in town. He first met fellow author and heavy drinker Ernest Hemingway at the former Dingo Bar in Montparnasse and later asked Hemingway to read *The Great Gatsby* at the nearby Closerie des Lilas. Alcohol would ultimately lead to Fitzgerald's ruin, destroying his health and ending his life at age forty-four.

Addresses for Fitzgerald

- Hôtel Ritz, 15, place Vendôme (1st)—first lodging for the family in Paris and home of the bar Fitzgerald introduced to Hemingway

- 14, rue de Tilsitt (8th)—the Fitzgeralds rented a fifth-floor apartment near the Arc de Triomphe in the mid-1920s

- Auberge de Venise, 10, rue Delambre (14th)—the former Dingo Bar, location of Fitzgerald's first meeting with Hemingway

- Harry's New York Bar, 5, rue Daunou (2nd)—another favorite bar

- Closerie des Lilas, 171, boulevard du Montparnasse (6th)—café where Fitzgerald asked Hemingway to read his newly published novel *The Great Gatsby*

- 58, rue de Vaugirard (6th)—site of the fourth-floor apartment the family lived in for six months in 1928 across from the Luxembourg Gardens; it became the model for Dick Diver's home in *Tender Is the Night*

- 3-5, rue Palatine (6th)—another address near the Luxembourg Gardens where the Fitzgeralds lived for two months in 1929;

the couple had a huge fight here after Zelda called Scott a "fairy"

Ernest Hemingway (1899-1961)

No revelation here: Hemingway loved Paris. In the posthumous memoir, *A Moveable Feast*, he compares living and working in the French capital to "having a great treasure given to you." So how did a young man from Oak Park, Illinois make his way to the sophisticated capital of France? The first step came when, instead of going to college, Hemingway took a job as a reporter for *The Kansas City Star*—a decision which helped develop his succinct writing style. While serving in the ambulance corps in Italy during World War I, he was severely wounded and sent home. A few years later with wife #1 Hemingway was back as the foreign correspondent for the *Toronto Star* in Paris. Having a letter of introduction from Sherwood Anderson, Hemingway met Gertrude Stein who invited him to her literary salon and became his mentor—for a while anyway, until the two outsized egos began clashing. A big drinker, Hemingway frequented Parisian cafés with fellow expat authors like Archie MacLeish, Ezra Pound, and Scott Fitzgerald. His marriage fell apart when Hemingway began an affair with Paris-based *Vogue* journalist Pauline Pfeiffer, who became the second of his four wives. One of the most celebrated American novelists, Hemingway was awarded the Nobel Prize for Literature in 1954. He committed suicide seven years later.

Addresses for Hemingway

- Hôtel d'Angleterre (then Hôtel Jacob), 44, rue Jacob (6th)— Hemingway and his first wife Hadley Richardson stayed at this location after arriving in Paris in 1921

- Le Pré aux Clercs, still open for business at 30, rue Bonaparte (6th)—restaurant near their hotel where the couple liked to eat out

- Café de la Paix, 12, boulevard des Capucines (9th)—site of their Christmas dinner splurge which sent Hemingway rushing home for more money to cover the bill

- 74, rue du Cardinal Lemoine (5th)—the couple's first apartment; notice the historical plaque which marks the building

- 39, rue Descartes (5th)—an attic room down the street which Hemingway rented to do his writing

- 27, rue de Fleurus (6th)—the address of Gertrude Stein's apartment where Hemingway attended her famous literary salon

- Dingo Bar, now Auberge de Venise, 10, rue Delambre (14th)—famous locale where Hemingway first met Scott Fitzgerald

- La Closerie des Lilas, 171, boulevard du Montparnasse (6th)—a bronze plaque indicates the author's preferred spot at the bar

- 113, rue Notre-Dame des Champs (6th)—the family rented an apartment above an old saw mill here; neither the business nor the address exists today

- 69, rue Froidevaux (14th)—address of the studio of Gerald and Sara Murphy; Hemingway stayed there after separating from Hadley in 1926

- 6, rue Ferou (6th)—Hemingway lived here with Pauline Pfeiffer, his second wife

- Hôtel Ritz, 15, place Vendôme (1st)—the famous luxury hotel where the author sometimes stayed and often drank with Fitzgerald; a bar in the hotel is now named after Hemingway

Langston Hughes (1902-1967)

Growing up in Joplin, Missouri the future poet had long imagined living in the French capital. In February 1924, while working on a merchant ship in Holland, Hughes hopped a train to Paris's Gare du Nord train station. Despite the freezing temperatures and having only seven dollars in his pocket, he described arriving in the city as "a dream come true." In his autobiography, *The Big Sea,* Hughes tells of the thrill of seeing the place Vendôme and the place de la Concorde for the first time and his gratitude for the heated galleries of the

Louvre. He enjoyed long walks in the forest at Versailles, going to the theater, and dancing at the Moulin Rouge with a young British woman he had met. More importantly, though, he felt that Paris was where "you can be whatever you want to be. Totally yourself." Every place has its drawbacks and for Hughes it was the post-World War I Parisians he called: "the most franc-loving, sou-clutching, hard-faced, hard-worked, cold and half-starved set of people I've ever seen." After dealing with belligerent crowds as a bouncer at the Cozy Corner nightclub in Montmartre, the mild-mannered Hughes moved on to a nearby club, Le Grand Duc, the inspiration for his poem, "Jazz Band in a Parisian Cabaret."

Addresses for Hughes

- Le Grand Duc, then at 52, rue Jean-Baptiste Pigalle (9th)—former cabaret where Hughes worked and first met Ada "Bricktop" Smith who was performing there; read more about Bricktop in Chapter 10

- 15, rue Nollet (17th)—Hughes's attic apartment before moving to a similar one on the rue des Trois Frères

- Moulin Rouge, 82, boulevard de Clichy (18th)—a dance spot he enjoyed with Anne Cousey, called "Mary" in his autobiography

- Opéra Comique, 1, place Boïeldieu (2nd)—where Hughes saw Manon with Alain Locke, the father of the Harlem Renaissance

- Café Palais Royal 202, rue Saint-Honoré (1st)—art collector Albert Barnes had lunch with Hughes here

Sinclair Lewis (1885-1951)

"Red" Lewis was the kind of guy who marched to the beat of a different drummer his whole life. Even growing up in Sauk Centre, Minnesota, the skinny, non-athletic, boy preferred solitary activities like reading and writing in his diary to playing sports or interacting with others. The practice he got writing obviously paid off and observations of his hometown provided the inspiration for his widely acclaimed novel, *Main Street*. True to character, Lewis rejected the Pulitzer Prize in 1926 for *Arrowsmith* because he felt that working for "alien rewards" instead of excellence was dangerous for authors. He had a change of heart a few years later, however, when he became the first American awarded the Nobel Prize for literature. Author of twenty-two novels, Lewis was as intense about his work as Balzac—often getting up to write in the middle of the night. An avid traveler as well as an alcoholic, Lewis spent extended periods in Paris writing and, of course, frequenting cafés. Snubbed by other literary expatriates such as Stein and Joyce for simply being a "best-selling author," Lewis did have a small group of friends in the French capital including American poet Ramon Guthrie. Sinclair Lewis died of advanced alcoholism just before his sixty-sixth birthday.

Addresses for Lewis

- Hôtel de Noailles (now the Hôtels Saint James et Albany), 202, rue de Rivoli (1st)—where Lewis worked on *Babbitt* during a stay in 1921

- Hôtel Élysée-Bellevue, 2, avenue Montaigne (8th)—four years later he wrote *Arrowsmith* at this former hotel

- rue de Varize (16th)—site of Lewis's 1927 apartment, number unknown

- Dingo Bar, now Auberge de Venise, 10, rue Delambre, as well as Le Dôme, 108, boulevard du Montparnasse (both in the 14th), Gypsy, once at 20, rue Cujas (5th), the Café Voltaire, 1, place de l'Odéon (6th) also closed, and Harry's New York Bar, still going strong at 5, rue Daunou (2nd)—watering holes favored by the author

Archibald MacLeish (1892-1982)

Though not very well known these days, "Archie" was quite an accomplished fellow. A pal of Hemingway and Stein, MacLeish was the recipient of three Pulitzer Prizes, the National Book Award, and an Academy Award. If that weren't enough, he also served as the Librarian of Congress. Like many of his generation, the Illinois native got his first view of France as an ambulance driver during World War I. After working for a few years as a lawyer in Boston, he resigned the day he was promoted to partner in order to devote time to his poetry. In September 1923 he and his wife, noted soprano Ada Hitchcock, took off for a five-year stay in Paris with their two young children. During his time in the French capital, MacLeish frequented Shakespeare and Company whose owner Sylvia Beach indirectly introduced him to Hemingway. The two friends were sparring partners for a while until MacLeish tired of getting pummeled by "Pappy," as he called the younger author. As was often the case with Hemingway, it was the beginning of a long and difficult friendship. In 1926 Pierpont Morgan Hamilton let the MacLeishes live rent-free in his luxury apartment, but paying the nine servants' salaries nearly ruined the family financially.

Addresses for MacLeish

- 23, rue las Cases (7th)—cramped first home of MacLeish and his family in Paris

- 85, boulevard Saint-Michel (5th)—the family's unheated, fourth-floor apartment across from the Luxembourg Gardens

- Brasserie Lipp, 151, boulevard Saint-Germain and Les Deux Magots, 6, place Saint Germain-des-Prés (both in the 6th)—two of MacLeish's favorite cafés

- 44, rue du Bac (7th)—a studio MacLeish rented which was once home to Picasso

- Shakespeare and Company, 12, rue de l'Odéon (6th)—site of Sylvia Beach's famous bookstore which MacLeish frequented

- 41, avenue du Bois de Boulogne, now the avenue Foch (16th)—location of Pierpont Morgan Hamilton's luxury apartment where the family lived rent-free for six weeks in 1926

- 14, rue Guynemer (6th)—the MacLeish family spent their last few months in the capital at this address near the Luxembourg Gardens

Edna St. Vincent Millay (1892-1950)

"My candle burns at both ends…," Millay famously wrote in her poem "First Fig." Like that metaphorical taper, her life had moments of tremendous brightness before burning out in a fall down stairs at age fifty-eight. Born in the coastal town of Rockland, Maine, young Vincent, as she preferred to be called, started writing a novel at age eight. By twenty she attracted national attention by failing to win the top prize in a poetry contest which many thought she deserved. After college at Vassar, Millay spent several years in Greenwich Village where she did some acting, published her first book, and had several amorous relationships. Once she was named foreign correspondent for *Vanity Fair* magazine in January 1921, Millay moved to the French capital, hoping to be "entirely alone." In Paris, however, she had many brief affairs, including with poet Edgar Lee Masters and sculptor Thelma Wood. Even though her platonic relationships in the city were few, Millay dined with Romanian artist Constantin Brancusi in his studio and posed for a picture by photographer Man Ray. Displeased with the photograph, however, she sent it home complaining that it was "pretty rotten, but never mind." In 1932 on a trial separation from her husband Millay again lived in Paris with a much younger man, fellow Pulitzer Prize-winning poet George Dillon.

Addresses for Millay

- Hôtel des Saints-Pères, 65, rue des Saints-Pères (7th)—Millay first spent a few months in a room at this hotel, still in operation

- Hôtel de l'Intendant de Paris, 11, rue de Vendôme (3rd)—she then moved to this former hotel on what is now the rue Béranger near place de la République

- 8, impasse Ronsin (15th)—Millay had dinner with sculptor Brancusi in his studio at this address

- Hôtel Vénétia, 159, boulevard du Montparnasse (6th)—Millay and her mother Cora lived at this hotel, no longer in business, in 1922

- La Rotonde, 105, boulevard du Montparnasse (6th)—Millay wrote back to her sister that "mummie & I come here every day & eat the stinkin' stuff" like onion soup

- Hôtel Pont Royal, 5-7, rue Montalembert (7th)—Millay and her lover George Dillon stayed here in 1932

- 5, rue Benjamin Godard (16th)—she then took an apartment in this fashionable section of the city

Ezra Pound (1885-1972)

Pound found fame as a Modernist poet and infamy as a proponent of fascism. He later called the fascist period of his life "a stupid suburban prejudice of anti-Semitism." An only child born in what was then called "Idaho Territory," Pound grew up in Philadelphia. He decided to become a poet at age eleven after getting a limerick published in a local newspaper. Eventually making his way to London, Pound met and married British artist Dorothy Shakespear. Once the couple moved to Paris in December 1920, Pound served as a writer and editor for Margaret Anderson's literary magazine *The Little Review*. He made a wide variety of friends in the French capital; these included members of the French Dada and Surrealist movements along with fellow Americans. In an interesting trade with Hemingway, Pound reviewed the younger writer's manuscripts in exchange for boxing lessons. Hemingway, however, complained that Pound had "the general grace of the crayfish" and "habitually leads with his chin." A generous man, besides editing other authors' works, Pound helped build shelves for Sylvia Beach's bookshop. After moving to Italy in 1924, he began writing anti-Semitic material. At a trial for treason in the U. S. in 1945, Pound was judged to be of unsound mind and spent twelve years in a psychiatric hospital in Washington D. C.

Addresses for Pound

- 92, rue Raynouard (16th)—Pound began working on *The Cantos* in 1911 and 1912 while staying in pianist Walter Rummel's spacious apartment in Passy

- 70 bis, rue Notre-Dame des Champs (6ᵗʰ)—location of the inexpensive, ground-floor apartment he shared with his wife Dorothy Shakespear, later rented by Katherine Anne Porter

- Le Dôme, 108, boulevard du Montparnasse (14ᵗʰ)—café where Pound often played chess with British novelist Ford Madox Ford

- 20, rue Jacob (6ᵗʰ)—he met his lifelong love American violinist Olga Rudge at Natalie Barney's famous literary salon in the fall of 1922

- Salle Pleyel, previously located at 22, rue de Rochechouart (9ᵗʰ)— where Pound staged his opera based on François Villon's *Le Testament* in 1924

Gertrude Stein (1874-1946)

The famous "A rose is a rose is a rose" writer was a witty, vain, and imposing figure in early twentieth-century Paris. From wealthy beginnings in Allegheny, Pennsylvania, she enjoyed advantages such as traveling in Europe with her family and studying at Radcliffe. In 1903 Stein abandoned medical studies at Johns Hopkins and moved to the Left Bank Parisian apartment of her brother Leo. The two siblings then began collecting avant-garde paintings and discussing them at their home with new-found friends like Matisse. The informal get-togethers grew steadily in popularity, eventually making their apartment "the place to be" Saturday evenings at nine. Such legendary people as Hemingway, Picasso, and Joyce gathered around the petite woman in her high-back Renaissance chair to gossip and talk about literature and art. After meeting Alice Toklas in 1907, Stein and her lifelong love began living together at the apartment. Seven years later Leo Stein left town because of what he termed his sister's "absurd notion of genius." Gertrude Stein acquired mainstream appeal for her writing with her 1933 book, *The Autobiography of Alice B. Toklas.* For a delightful look at this period, check out Hemingway's memoir, *A Moveable Feast,* and Woody

Allen's film, *Midnight in Paris,* with Kathy Bates in the role of Stein.

Addresses for Stein

- 27, rue de Fleurus (6ᵗʰ)—the site of Stein's celebrated literary salon, marked with a white historical plaque, is found near the west entrance to the Luxembourg Gardens

- 5, rue Christine (6ᵗʰ)—after leaving town during World War I Stein and Toklas settled in an apartment at this address near the quai des Grands Augustins

- Père Lachaise, 16, rue du Repos (20ᵗʰ)—burial place of the couple near the rue des Rondeaux, métro Gambetta

Glenway Wescott (1901-1987)

Even the very well read might not recognize this writer's name. But in his youth the Milwaukee-born Wescott gained recognition for his works by big names such as Wallace Stevens, William Carlos Williams, and Sinclair Lewis. *The Grandmothers*, a novel published when he was just twenty-four, was described as "almost Flaubertian" by one critic. No small praise, indeed. Wescott's early successes, however, weren't maintained because of fear of failure, lack of discipline, and a keen propensity for partying. In 1925 Wescott obtained a publisher's advance, plus a gift from a wealthy American, and traveled to France with his partner, Monroe Wheeler. The couple enjoyed Paris but, finding the city distracting and expensive, spent three years in a fishing village near Nice. Once back in the French capital Wescott became part of the expatriate literary and artistic community which included Katherine Anne Porter, Janet Flanner, and Isadora Duncan. He attended the salon of Gertrude Stein who said enigmatically that the young man "has a certain syrup but it does not pour." Hemingway, a jealous, homophobic type, scorned his fellow author's affectations and undoubtedly fumed when his own mother suggested that he should write more like Wescott. Wescott's final triumph came with the 1940 novella,

The Pilgrim Hawk, hailed by writer Susan Sontag as a treasure of twentieth-century American literature.

Addresses for Wescott

- Hôtel Savoy, 30, rue de Vaugirard (6th)—former hotel where the author worked on his story, *Fire and Water*

- 218, boulevard Raspail (14th)—Wescott and Wheeler rented "a miserably inconvenient flat" for three months at this address

- 32, rue de Vaugirard (6th)—previous apartment of Wheeler's publishing partner Barbara Harrison where the two men stayed in September 1929

- 9, rue de Condé (6th)—the following year Wescott and Wheeler moved to this apartment near the place de l'Odéon

Thornton Wilder (1897-1975)

Gregariousness, friendly, and curious, Wilder was interested in a wide mix of people and subjects. His experiences and insight led him to become the first author to win Pulitzer Prizes for both drama and fiction. As a youth in a strict Calvinist household in Madison, Wisconsin, he turned to composing stories and plays. His first publication, *The Trumpet Shall Sound*, appeared in the literary magazine at Yale. While teaching at a New Jersey prep school, he was hired by parents to take their struggling son to Europe in 1926. As part of that trip, Wilder befriended Fitzgerald, Hemingway, and Glenway Wescott, among others in Paris. After the student returned home, Wilder could have moved into a studio with Hemingway—who was going through a divorce from his first wife—but wisely chose to stay elsewhere. As a professor at the University of Chicago, Wilder attended a lecture by Gertrude Stein in 1934 which led to a long friendship. In a letter to Stein, often his literary critic, Wilder once coyly wrote: "Oh, what fun it is to be cudgeled by Gertrude, to be enlightened, and slapped, and warmed, and crushed, and slain, and brought alive by Gertrude," A closeted gay man, he apparently feared his homosexuality would ruin his reputation and his career.

Addresses for Wilder

- Hôtel du Maroc, once located at 57, rue de Seine (6th)—the June 1921 residence of Wilder until his departure was hastened by bedbugs

- Hôtel Édouard VII, at 39, avenue de l'Opéra (2nd)—lavish hotel, still in operation today, where he stayed with his student in 1926

- Schola Cantorum at 269, rue Saint-Jacques (5th)—Wilder began working on his Pulitzer Prize-winning best-seller, *The Bridge of San Luis Rey,* in a pension at this address

- Hôtel Buckingham, 43, rue des Mathurins (8th)—he took a room at this former hotel in 1935 and again four years later

- Brasserie Lipp, 151, boulevard Saint-Germain (6th)—restaurant where Wilder dined with theatrical producer Jed Harris

- 20, rue Jacob (6th)—site of Natalie Barney's "very brilliant" literary salon which he visited in 1939

William Carlos Williams (1883-1963)

A poet and a pediatrician, Williams became so enthralled with the French capital that he actually considered relocating his medical practice there. Williams was no stranger to Europe; he had been a schoolboy in Geneva and Paris for several years. While studying medicine at the University of Pennsylvania, he began a lifelong friendship with Ezra Pound who greatly influenced his poetry. Although he led a mainly conventional doctor's life in his hometown of Rutherford, New Jersey, at the encouragement of Pound, Williams decided to take a sabbatical. So in January 1924 he and his wife Flossie left for Europe and spent a total of six weeks in Paris. The couple's whirlwind tour of the city included museums, plays, and galleries as well as meeting Romanian sculptor Constantin Brancusi at his studio and having dinner with Irish author James Joyce. Through friends like author

Bob McAlmon and Pound, Williams was also introduced to a variety of American artists and writers such as Man Ray, Djuna Barnes, Gertrude Stein, and Ernest Hemingway. The insecure doctor/poet felt scorned at times by old friends Pound and Hilda Doolittle, yet he was especially charmed by the "unflinching kindness" of bookseller Adrienne Monnier and her partner Sylvia Beach of Shakespeare and Company fame.

Addresses for Williams

- 42, rue La Bruyère (9ᵗʰ)—after leaving Geneva for Paris the teenager lived with his mother and brother at the home of cousins at this address near place Pigalle in Montmartre

- Lycée Condorcet. 8, rue du Havre (9ᵗʰ)—the boys attended this high school for a short while until they decided their French wasn't sufficient for classes there

- Hôtel Lutetia, 45, boulevard Raspail (6ᵗʰ)—author Bob McAlmon reserved a room for Williams and his wife at this luxury hotel in 1924

- Au Vieux Colombier, 65, rue de Rennes (6ᵗʰ)—still in operation, this restaurant is where the couple had dinner on their first night in Paris

- Le Dôme, 108, boulevard Montparnasse (14ᵗʰ)—Williams saw his friend Ezra Pound and met Hemingway at this café

- 113, rue Notre-Dame des Champs (6ᵗʰ)—apartment of Hadley and Ernest Hemingway where Dr. Williams circumcised their baby; neither the building nor the street number still exists

- Dingo Bar (now renamed Auberge de Venise) at 10, rue Delambre (14ᵗʰ) and the Les Deux Magots, 6, place Saint-Germain-des-Prés (6ᵗʰ)—other favorite hang-outs for the Williamses

- Hôtel Istria, 29, rue Campagne Première (14ᵗʰ)—where the couple had a room on a return trip to the city in 1927

Chapter 6

From the Great Depression to the Present (Fiction Writers after 1930)

WRITERS, WRITERS EVERYWHERE! RESEARCHING Americans who have lived in Paris, I found that authors of fiction are by far the largest group. Beginning around 1930 many highly creative men and women reacted to oppressive conditions at home—including prohibition, the Great Depression, racism, and homophobia—by rushing toward the freedom, avant-garde ideas, and tolerance of the French capital city. The following pages list some of the most prominent among them from James Baldwin to Richard Wright.

James Baldwin (1924-1987)

"Jimmy," as he was known to friends, revealed a knack for writing in early childhood. His talent was recognized by author Richard Wright who helped the younger man get a grant to fulfill his long-time dream of living in Paris. Arriving with just forty dollars in his pocket, Baldwin had no choice but to adopt the Cheapo lifestyle. His description of the low-priced rooms says it all: "Paris hotels had never heard of central heating or hot baths or clean towels and sheets or ham and eggs." While not exactly enamored of the French either, Baldwin didn't feel the discrimination of back home. In fact, he found an atmosphere where he could develop into a real writer, and not, as he put it, "merely a Negro writer." Equally important perhaps, he was able to live without fear as an openly gay man. Fueled by coffee and cognac, Baldwin discussed literature with friends and revised most of his novel, *Go Tell It on the Mountain,* upstairs at the Café de Flore. For the last seventeen years of his life, Baldwin lived in the south of France with his partner, American dancer Bernard Hassell. The year before his death his adopted country honored Baldwin by bestowing on him its highest award, the Légion d'honneur.

Addresses for Baldwin

- Hôtel de Verneuil, 8, rue de Verneuil (7th)—a now chic, formerly shabby hotel where the author once lived

- Le Café de Flore, 172, boulevard Saint-Germain, Les Deux Magots, 6, place Saint-Germain-des-Prés, and Brasserie Lipp, 151, boulevard Saint-Germain (all in the 6th)—three of the big Saint-Germain cafés which Baldwin patronized

- Pergola Lounge, 70, rue Rocher (8th)—another favorite bar, recently renamed L'Envers du Décor

- Le Tournon, at 18, rue de Tournon (6th)—this café attracted many African-Americans of the period, including Baldwin until he found the location less than gay-friendly and had a falling out with Dick Wright

Saul Bellow (1915-2005)

For some, Saul Bellow was a "tough," "difficult" man, but few could deny his talent. Winner of both the Pulitzer and Nobel Prizes, he was born in Lachine, Quebec to Russian immigrant parents who moved the family to Chicago. After making his mark in the literary world with two early novels, Bellow was granted a Guggenheim fellowship and moved with his first wife and young son to Paris in 1948. In a small hotel room a short walk from their apartment the author found his literary voice writing the novel, *The Adventures of Augie March,* which would win the National Book Award. During his two years in the French capital, Bellow developed a love/hate relationship with the city and its people. On one hand, he was *aux anges* (in heaven) wandering the streets and relaxing at cafés with friends; yet he detested the infamous gray skies of Northern Europe which were "devoid of any brightness." Likewise, Bellow admired the great French authors of the past but openly disdained ordinary citizens whom he described as curmudgeonly, gloomy, proud, and anti-Semitic. The French, for their part, appreciated Bellow's writing and in 1968 awarded him *la Croix de Chevalier des Arts et Lettres* (Cross of the Knight of Arts and Letters) for significant contributions to literature.

Addresses for Bellow

- 11, rue Vaneau (7th)—site of the small apartment taken by Bellow and family when they first arrived in Paris
- 33, rue Vaneau (7th)—they soon found more suitable accommodations just down the street
- Hôtel de l'Académie [Saint Germain], 32, rue des Saints-Pères (7th)—the author rented a room at this hotel to do his writing
- Le Rouquet, 188, boulevard Saint-Germain (7th)—one of Bellow's favorite cafés, still open for business

William S. Burroughs (1914-1997)

That Bill Burroughs lived to the ripe old age of eighty-three is nothing short of a miracle. Poet Allen Ginsberg once accurately described his friend as having a "startling penchant for wildness." This tendency toward risky behavior began when, as a high schooler in the suburbs of St. Louis, Burroughs began playing around with knives, firearms, and drugs. This volatile mix would come back to haunt him in the years to come. Working as a copywriter for an advertising agency in New York, he met Beat Generation authors Ginsberg and Jack Kerouac. Although often romantically involved with men, during this time Burroughs began a long-term relationship with Beat poet Joan

Vollmer. Fleeing drugs and weapons charges in New Orleans, the couple settled in Mexico City where Burroughs shot and killed his twenty-eight-year-old partner in a William Tell reenactment, perhaps accidentally. An itinerant period followed and in 1959 he moved to the so-called "Beat Hotel" on the Left Bank of the French capital. Burroughs then secured a Paris-based publisher for his best-known novel, *Naked Lunch*, considered obscene at the time in the U.S. Involved with drugs in Paris, Burroughs was regularly tracked by French police for possible opium smuggling but was never jailed on charges.

Addresses for Burroughs

- 9, rue Gît-le-Cœur (6th)—former rooming house that Burroughs, Ginsberg, and Greg Corso termed the "Beat Hotel;" now the respectable Relais Hôtel du Vieux Paris with a plaque indicating its notorious past

- Shakespeare and Company, 37, rue de la Bûcherie (5th)—the Whitman bookstore, still in operation, that the author enjoyed visiting

- La Palette 43, rue de Seine (6th)—a one-time drug-dealing center and favorite haunt of Burroughs, open for business today

Lawrence Ferlinghetti (1919-)

Some think that San Francisco's City Lights bookstore was named as a tribute to Paris. Could be. Larry Ferlinghetti, its owner and creator, spent four years in the French capital before becoming a well-known poet, painter, publisher, and political activist. Born to the Ferling family in Yonkers, New York, he later restored the original family name. The young boy had a very difficult start in life. Arriving in the world after his father's death and just before his mother was institutionalized, he was bounced around among caretakers. Finally, his Aunt Émilie took him under her wing and moved with him to her native Alsace. Fluent in French from his years abroad, Ferlinghetti chose to pursue a doctorate in creative writing at the Sorbonne. Once settled in Paris in 1947, he found a stash of art supplies in his apartment and signed up for painting classes at the Académie Julian. During his time in the city he courted his future wife, enjoyed the opera, and frequented the cafés of Saint-Germain and Montparnasse. Long discussions with his friend George Whitman led Whitman to open a bookstore on the Left Bank and perhaps inspired Ferlinghetti to do the same years later in California. The first Poet Laureate of San Francisco, his classic collection, *A Coney Island of the Mind,* is one of the best-selling books of American poetry.

Addresses for Ferlinghetti

- 2, place Voltaire (11th)—later renamed place Léon Blum—Ferlinghetti improved his language skills living with the Letellier family

- 89, rue de Vaugirard (6th)—location of his damp basement apartment in Montparnasse where he discovered art supplies and began painting

- 37, rue de la Bûcherie (5th)—still in operation, Whitman's Shakespeare and Company, originally called Le Mistral, was renamed in honor of Sylvia Beach's famous bookstore; Whitman often welcomed Ferlinghetti to his store and provided him a place to stay upstairs on his return visits to the city

- Café Mabillon, 164, boulevard Saint-Germain (6th)—a favorite hangout of the author and his future wife Kirby

Chester Himes (1909-1984)

"The father of Black American crime writing" ironically made his entrance into the literary world after becoming a criminal himself. Born to middle-class teachers in Jefferson City, Missouri, Himes committed a series of wrongdoings as a young man and was eventually convicted of armed robbery. While in confinement at the Ohio State Penitentiary, he wrote short stories and published an article in *Esquire* magazine using his prison number as a "pseudonym." In the early 1950s Himes decided to leave his home country as well as his first wife and head for Paris. The French capital, unlike New York, he once said, "allowed me to live and get ahead." So much about expatriate life in the French capital appealed to Himes, especially escape from racial prejudice, respect for his writing, and friendship with authors like James Baldwin and Richard Wright. To earn a better living, Himes took the suggestion of an editor at Gallimard Press to start producing detective novels. Four of his books—including *If He Hollers Let Him Go* and *Cotton Comes to Harlem*—were subsequently made into films for the American market. To honor his work the French government awarded Himes France's Grand Prix de la littérature policière (Grand Prize of the Mystery Novel) in 1958.

Addresses for Himes

- Hôtel Delavigne at 1, rue Casimir Delavigne, Hôtel Michelet, 6, place de l'Odéon, and Hôtel Rachou, later called Beat Hotel (now Relais Hôtel Vieux Paris), 9, rue Gît-le-Cœur (all in the 6th)—cheap hotels where Himes stayed when he first arrived in the capital

- Le Tournon, 20, rue Tournon (6th)—a favorite hang-out for Himes, Wright, and many other African-American writers, artists, and musicians

- Hôtel Welcome at 66, rue de Seine (6th)—Himes rented a room in this hotel after filming a documentary in Harlem

- 3, rue Bourbon-le-Château (6th)—a top-floor studio where he lived with his second wife and wrote *A Rage in Harlem*

- 132, rue d'Assas (6th)—the couple moved to this address when the other apartment's lease ran out

- 21, rue de l'Estrapade (5th)—Himes and his wife stayed here for a month on a return trip after moving to Spain

Douglas Kennedy (1955-):

"Douglas who?" you might be wondering about now. Hard to fathom but this internationally known, best-selling author keeps a very low profile in his home country. So low that in 2010 *Time* magazine appropriately called him "the most famous American writer you never heard of." Kennedy's novels have been translated into over twenty languages but he is better known in the U.S. for films based on them such as *The Woman in the Fifth*. From the Upper West Side of Manhattan, Kennedy studied at Bowdoin College in Maine, spending his junior year at Dublin's Trinity College. The self-described "globalist" moved to Ireland after graduation, working as an administrator at a theatre during the day and doing his writing at night. After publishing a travel account on Egypt, Kennedy decided to devote himself entirely to his own work and moved to London. He also rented a small studio on the top floor of an old brothel in Paris. Since then he changed to better living quarters on rue de Lancry near the Canal Saint-Martin (10th). In 2007 France showed Kennedy its appreciation by awarding him the highest literary distinction given to non-citizens: Chevalier de l'Ordre des Arts et des Lettres ("Knight of Arts and Letters"). Two years later he received the *Figaro* newspaper's Grand Prix for literature.

Addresses for Kennedy

- Le Café de Flore, 172, boulevard Saint-Germain (6th), Chez Prune, 36, rue Beaurepaire, and the restaurant of the Hôtel du Nord 102, quai des Jemmapes (both in the 10th)—Kennedy's favorite cafés and writing spots

Henry Miller (1891-1980)

"Born to be wild" is how one blogger describes Miller. Let's just say that much of the material for his novels, banned for overt sexuality in the 30s, sprang from his chosen lifestyle. The son of German immigrants in Manhattan, Miller was an excellent student but abandoned his studies at City College after a few months. He initially traveled to Paris in 1928 with his second wife June. After their divorce, Miller decided to move to the French capital to devote all of his time to writing. Having very little money at the beginning of his stay, he led a miserable existence "on the bum," living with friends in twenty-five or so different places over three years. During four months at a fellow writer's apartment in Montparnasse, Miller began composing *Tropic of Cancer*. In the novel a character—perhaps expressing Miller's own views—declares his disappointment with the French capital: "Paris is like a whore. From a distance she seems ravishing…five minutes later you feel empty, disgusted with yourself." Still, he made the city home for ten years and enjoyed, among other things, the grand cafés along the boulevard du Montparnasse and the farmers' market on boulevard Edgar-Quinet (14th). Once the author became the lover of diarist Anaïs Nin, he no longer had financial worries and moved into his own place in Montparnasse.

Addresses for Miller

- Hôtel de Paris at 24, rue Bonaparte (6th) and Grand Hôtel des Écoles (now the Lenox Montparnasse) at 15, rue Delambre (14th)—where Miller and second wife June stayed in 1928

- 2, rue Auguste-Bartholdi (15th)—lawyer Richard Osborn welcomed the author to spend the winter of 1930-31 at his studio in a seventh-floor walk-up at this address

- Villa Seurat, 101, rue de la Tombe Issoire (14th)—in 1931 Miller spent time writing *Tropic of Cancer* at a friend's home at #18 of this cul-de-sac and later had his own apartment in the same building

- Le Sphinx at 31, boulevard Edgar Quinet (14th)—site of a former brothel Miller frequented

- Hôtel Central at 1, bis, rue du Maine (14th)—Miller shared a room here with Alfred Perlès and had his first tryst with Anaïs Nin in room 40 of this hotel

- 4, rue Anatole France (17th)—the two men later moved to this address

- *Chicago Herald Tribune*, 5, rue Lamartine (9th)—Miller took a job as a proofreader for this newspaper earning twelve dollars a week

- Petit Poucet at 5, place Clichy (8th) and the Brasserie Wepler, 14, place de Clichy (18th)—two favorite writing spots for Miller, both still in business today

Katherine Anne Porter (1890-1980)

Although supposedly descended from "American royalty"—the likes of pioneer Daniel Boone and author O. Henry—Callie Russell Porter had a rough start in life. She was born in a log cabin in Indian Creek, Texas, just two years before the death of her mother. Her father then neglected the children...which some believe led Porter to a lifelong search for love through multiple marriages and affairs. Raised by her grandmother, whose name she eventually adopted as her own, the young girl was passionate about reading and writing. Her first volume of short stories, *Flowering Judas and Other Stories* (1930), won her a Guggenheim fellowship for study abroad. After spending the winter in Berlin, she went on to Paris, a city she loved "on sight and without reservation." In the French capital Porter befriended bookstore owners Sylvia Beach and Adrienne Monnier, publishers Barbara Harrison and Monroe Wheeler, and Wheeler's partner author Glenway Wescott. In 1933 Porter met Hemingway at Shakespeare and Company but Beach wounded his male ego when she compared the unknown female author favorably to him. Porter began or worked on her most famous pieces while living in Paris, including the novel *Ship of Fools* which was based on a journal she started while sailing to Europe. She was awarded the Pulitzer Prize for fiction in 1966.

Addresses for Porter

- Hôtel Malherbe, formerly located on the Left Bank at 11, rue de Vaugirard (6th)—Porter's first lodging in the capital

- Hôtel Savoy once found at 30, rue de Vaugirard (6th)—where she lived for a month in 1932 before subletting her friend, British author, Ford Madox Ford's apartment next door at number 32

- Les Deux Magots, 6, place Saint Germain-des-Prés (6th)—Porter and Eugene Pressly popped champagne with the Fords, Beach, and Monnier at this café to celebrate their 1933 marriage

- 166, boulevard du Montparnasse (14th)—the "roomy birdcage," as Porter called it, a top-floor apartment she and Pressly moved into a month after their wedding

- 70 bis, Notre-Dame des Champs (6th)—Ezra Pound's old six-room apartment where the couple lived from 1934 to 1936

John Steinbeck (1902-1968)

Believe it or not, before computers, authors had other ways of composing their works. Steinbeck, for his part, was the undisputed champion of the pencil. He went through forty to sixty a day—and supposedly used over three hundred for his voluminous novel *East of Eden*. The effort was not in vain, of course. The 1962 Nobel laureate is known worldwide for works such as *The Grapes of Wrath* and *Of Mice and Men*. Growing up in Salinas, California, Steinbeck observed the agricultural valley and the difficulties of migrant life. After his first marriage he decided to focus full time on writing and achieved critical success with *Tortilla Flat* in 1935. Steinbeck and his third (and final) wife began traveling the world in the early '50s and were especially impressed with the beauty of Paris. The author wrote that he thought Parisians were "the luckiest people in the world." He felt fortunate to spend an extended period in the city with his family in 1954. From his lavish residence across from the French president's Élysée Palace he wrote home: "How's that for a Salinas kid?" During those five months in the French capital he contributed a series of articles to the *Figaro* newspaper's literary magazine with the running title "One American in Paris."

Addresses for Steinbeck

- Hôtel Lancaster, 7, rue de Berri (8th)—site of the couple's lodging on their trip to Paris in 1952

- Jules Verne, avenue Gustave Eiffel (7th)—he and his wife dined at this exclusive restaurant on the second level of the Eiffel Tower

- 1, avenue de Marigny (8th)—an impressive five-story townhouse across from the French president's official residence where the Steinbecks lived for five months in 1954

Richard Wright (1908-1960)

It's hard to keep a good man down…certainly in Dick Wright's case at least. Starting life as a black sharecropper's son in rural Mississippi and having to relocate multiple times after his father deserted the family, nothing held the young boy back. Despite many challenges in his early life, Wright got a story printed in a local newspaper while still in his teens and went on to graduate as valedictorian of his junior high school class. He would, of course, eventually become an internationally renowned author. Living in New York in the late 1930s, he got his short story collection, *Uncle Tom's Children*, published and received a fellowship from the Guggenheim Foundation. Wright then achieved near celebrity status for his novel, *Native Son*, and memoir, *Black Boy*. Gertrude Stein, who appreciated Wright's work, was instrumental in getting him formally invited to Paris by the French government in May 1946. The author was immediately delighted by the beauty of the city and, perhaps even more so, by the fact that there was "no race-tension or conflict…no social snobbery." After a racial incident back home involving his daughter, Wright decided to move his family to the French capital in August of the following year. Both Martin Luther King, Jr. and Langston Hughes visited the author there shortly before his untimely death. Wright is buried in Père Lachaise Cemetery.

Addresses for Wright

- Trianon Palace Hotel, 3, rue de Vaugirard (3rd)—in May 1946 Stein reserved a room for Wright at this hotel still in operation near the Luxembourg Gardens

- 38, boulevard Saint-Michel (5th)—Wright and his family lived in a small apartment at this address in the summer of 1946

- Brasserie Balzar, 49, rue des Écoles (5th)—a favorite nearby dining spot for the author and his wife

- Chez Honey, rue Jules Chaplain [number unknown] (6th)—former art gallery/jazz club run by African-American Herb Gentry where Wright brought Sartre and Beauvoir on occasion

- Le Procope, 13, rue de l'Ancienne Comédie (6th)—he also enjoyed stopping in at the oldest café in Paris

- 9, rue de Lille near rue des Saints-Pères (7th)—first address for the Wrights where they lived for four months after moving to the city in August 1947

- 14, rue Monsieur-Le-Prince (6th)—the family settled here for several years; a white historical plaque marks the building

- Café Monaco (now the Le Comptoir du Relais), 9, Carrefour de l'Odéon and Le Tournon, at 20, rue de Tournon (both in the 6th)—Wright frequented the Monaco before switching definitively to the Tournon near the Luxembourg Gardens, referred to as "Dick's place" by friends like Chester Himes and James Baldwin

- 4, rue Régis (6th)—Wright moved to a small apartment at this address near Saint-Placide after living for a short time in London

- Père Lachaise, 16, rue du Repos (20th)—Wright's ashes are interred in this cemetery

Chapter 7

Journalists and Other Literary Figures

AUTHORS OF FICTION ARE not the only members of the literary world who flocked to Paris over the years. A wide-ranging group of other expatriates—journalists, editors, publishers, essayists—also made their living by the printed word in the French capital. Journalist Janet Flanner, for example, wins the prize for spending nearly fifty years in city hotels while she produced her famed column for *The New Yorker* magazine. Longtime editors and publishers of *The Little Review*, Margaret Anderson, and *The Paris Review*, George Plimpton, had residences as well as offices in the City of Light. Some of the writers included here, such as Ralph Waldo Emerson and Susan Sontag, dabbled in fiction but their "real jobs" as essayists make them better suited to this category. Contemporary humorist David Sedaris, who used his fractured French as the basis for the title essay in *Me Talk Pretty One Day*, seemingly retraced the path of other well-known jokesters like Dorothy Parker and Art Buchwald. Among the rest we find the founder of the legendary bookstore Shakespeare and Company Sylvia Beach, herself a critic, publisher, and translator. In total, eleven important figures make up this chapter.

Margaret Anderson (1886-1973)

Crane, Doolittle, Eliot, Stein, and Williams are but a few of the big-name authors whose works were published in *The Little Review*. Its creator, Margaret Anderson, got the idea for an avant-garde literary magazine in 1914 while working as a book critic for the *Chicago Evening Post*. The Indianapolis native, using the motto "Making No Compromise with the Public Taste," soon learned the ramifications of such a philosophy. She and her lover/co-editor Jane Heap were put on trial in New York for obscenity after publishing parts of James Joyce's *Ulysses* in 1921. But that didn't stop Anderson who friends described as "the born enemy of convention and discipline." After falling in love with French soprano Georgette LeBlanc, Anderson relocated to Paris and took the magazine with her. Living in the French capital, the couple was surrounded by members of the literary set which included Hemingway, Pound, and Janet Flanner. Like some other Americans, Anderson wrote that she was "repelled by the French," one assumes with the exception of LeBlanc in her case. But she did enjoy seeing "the chief enchantments" of the city—the Seine, the Louvre, Notre Dame, the Tuileries—by simply walking out of the Gare d'Orsay train station. Eventually, though, Anderson and LeBlanc moved south to Le Cannet on the French Rivera where both are buried.

Addresses for Anderson

- Hôtel Beaujolais, 15, rue de Beaujolais (1ˢᵗ)—in 1923 Anderson and LeBlanc first stayed at this former hotel behind the Palais Royal

- 22, rue de Grenelle (7ᵗʰ)—the address bookstore owner Sylvia Beach had in her register for Margaret Anderson

- 80, rue de l'Université (7ᵗʰ)—the couple rented a small apartment here

- Le Select, 99, boulevard du Montparnasse (6ᵗʰ)—Anderson patronized this café where she saw Hemingway pushing through terrace chairs looking for friends every morning

- 17, rue Casimir Périer (7th)—Anderson and LeBlanc had an apartment at this address near Les Invalides in 1936 and 1937

Sylvia Beach (1887-1962)

The legendary bookstore Shakespeare and Company only shares its name with the one currently found at 37, rue de la Bûcherie (5th). The original was created by a minister's daughter from Princeton, New Jersey: Sylvia Beach. While studying French literature at the Sorbonne in 1919, Beach met French bookseller Adrienne Monnier and got the idea of selling and lending English-language books in the city. From the start Shakespeare and Company was more than a simple bookstore. A long list of international authors—from Ezra Pound, Ernest Hemingway, and Ford Madox Ford to James Joyce—flocked to this intellectual center to read and discuss literature, and sometimes even get works printed; to pick up mail and arrange for typists; or to seek Beach's opinion on their writings. In 1922 she took the controversial step of publishing James Joyce's novel *Ulysses*, considered obscene at the time. When financial problems hit in the mid-30s, French novelist André Gide organized Friends of Shakespeare and Company to save it from closing. Trivial "infractions" during the Nazi Occupation resulted in Beach's one-month confinement with other women at the zoo in the Bois de Boulogne (16th). She was then sent to a prison camp in northeast France for six months. Beach spent the rest of her life in Paris but never reopened the bookstore after World War II.

Addresses for Beach

- Bibliothèque Nationale, 58, rue de Richelieu (2nd)—Beach was doing research at this library in 1917 when she came across the name of Adrienne Monnier's bookstore/lending library, La Maison des Amis des Livres then located at 7, rue de l'Odéon (6th)

- 8, rue Dupuytren (6th)—Beach first opened a small version of Shakespeare and Company at this address with the financial support of her mother and Monnier

- 12, rue de l'Odéon (6th)—the bookstore was relocated to larger premises across the street from Monnier's shop in May 1921; a white plaque marks the building

Art Buchwald (1925-2007)

The famed newspaperman and humorist found love and happiness during his fourteen years in Paris. He wrote: "Whoever goes there takes away the greatest meal he has ever had in his life, a romance that will linger forever, and a dream that will never be repeated." Life wasn't always so rosy for the Mount Vernon, New York native. Like many funnymen, Buchwald's sad childhood spent mainly in foster homes probably served as the impetus for his turn to humor. He penned a comic newsletter while serving in the Marines and later wrote for the college newspaper at Southern Cal. When he learned he could take classes abroad on the G.I. bill, Buchwald packed up and headed for the City of Light in June 1948. After cajoling his way into a position with the *International Herald Tribune*, he wrote a column called "Paris After Dark." One of his most popular articles purported to explain American Thanksgiving to Parisians by translating associated terms into broken French—like *Kilomètres Deboutish* for Miles Standish. In 1959 Buchwald had an extended interview with Elvis Presley and later recalled taking "the King" out to a cabaret. A funny, touching account of his days in the French capital, *I'll Always Have Paris*, was published in 1996.

Addresses for Buchwald

- Alliance Française, 101, boulevard Raspail (6th)—Buchwald attended French classes here, but even after fourteen years in Paris his language skills remained, shall we say, at a minimum

- Hôtel des États-Unis, formerly located at 135, boulevard du Montparnasse (14th)—he had a room at this address for seven dollars a week which included breakfast

- *International Herald Tribune* once found at 21, rue de Berri (8th)—Buchwald came up with the idea of writing an entertainment column for this newspaper called "Paris After Dark"

- Hôtel Plaza-Athénée, 25, avenue Montaigne (8th)—chic hotel where Buchwald met his wife, American author and publicist Ann McGarry

- 24, rue du Boccador (8th)—for a time the couple lived in a top-floor studio off the avenue George V

- 83, quai d'Orsay (7th)—he and his wife spent four years in a ground floor one-bedroom apartment here

- 52, rue de Monceau (8th)—the couple and their 3 adopted children lived at this address near the park of the same name

- Le Lido, 116 bis, avenue des Champs-Élysées (8th)—where Buchwald recalled bringing Elvis after their interview in 1959

Angela Davis (1944-)

Growing up in a section of Birmingham called "Dynamite Hill" is bound to have a lifelong influence on you. This was certainly the case for Davis who witnessed firsthand some of the racially-motivated bombings which gave the area its label. Far from paralyzed by the experience, however, Davis went on to become a prominent author, activist, and philosophy professor. The young woman got the chance to see parts of the world outside of Alabama after receiving a university scholarship to Brandeis. Following her first year in college, Davis took a trip to the French capital. She spent a few days in a hotel in the Latin Quarter before moving to a sixth-floor *chambre de bonne* (maid's room) close to the Eiffel Tower. As a French major, she returned to France during her junior year. That September, on a month-long preliminary program in Biarritz, she heard the shocking news about the church bombing which took the lives of four young girls in her hometown. In Paris Davis lived with a local family not far from the Arc de Triomphe. Thanks to her superior level of French, she was allowed to take classes alongside native-speakers at the Sorbonne. Her fluency in the language was still evident in the 1975 interview she gave about her autobiography on the former prime-time French television talk show *Apostrophes*.

Addresses for Davis

- 27 bis, rue Duret (16th)—during her junior year abroad Davis and another young American lived with a French family at this address behind the Arc de Triomphe
- Reid Hall, 4, rue de Chevreuse (6th)—former location of the study abroad offices for the Hamilton College program that Davis attended

Ralph Waldo Emerson (1803-1882)

His poor Massachusetts family which prized education gave Emerson the foundation to become the "sage of Concord." Growing up without a father from age eight, Emerson was influenced by his Aunt Mary, a well-read woman whose aphorisms like "Always do what you are afraid to do" he would later repeat to his own children. In 1829 the Harvard graduate became associate minister of Second Church in Boston. When his wife died a short time later, Emerson sailed to Malta and worked his way north to Paris by the spring of 1833. At first he was "very little enamored of the gay city." Yet, Emerson met with Lafayette, attended lectures at the Sorbonne, and visited Notre-Dame and the Louvre. Sure, he also enjoyed café life but came to regard the French capital as "a loud, modern New York of a place." But the city's Jardin des Plantes proved to be an epiphany for the young man and might have changed his opinion of the French capital for good. In this garden the future essayist, poet, and philosopher first realized "a correspondence between the human soul and everything that exists in the world." Emerson returned to Paris on two later occasions: after a lecture tour of England in 1848 and again with his daughter Ellen in 1873.

Addresses for Emerson

- Hôtel de Montmorency-Luxembourg (2nd)—in 1833 Emerson spent about a month at this hotel which once stretched from 11, boulevard Montmartre to 10, rue Saint-Marc, now the Passage des Panoramas; he also spent a short time here in 1848

- Jardin des Plantes, 57, rue Cuvier, (5ᵗʰ)—Emerson's first philosophical work, *Nature*, was inspired by visits to this botanical garden

- 15, rue des Petits Augustins, now the rue Bonaparte (6ᵗʰ)—on a lecture tour 1848 he took a room here; the building has been replaced

- Hôtel de France et de Lorraine, 7, rue de Beaune (7ᵗʰ)—Emerson stayed at this former hotel in March 1873

Janet Flanner (1892-1978)

After Gertrude Stein the most sought-after American in early twentieth century Paris was the witty, sophisticated author of *Letter from Paris*. Harold Ross creator of *The New Yorker* had recruited Flanner for his fledgling magazine and coined the name *Genêt* for her, thinking it sounded like a French version of Janet. Her writing career had begun as the art and drama columnist for her hometown paper, the *Indianapolis Star*. While living in Manhattan in 1918, Flanner met Solita Solano (née Sarah Wilkinson), drama editor for the *New York Tribune*, who became her longtime lover. The couple arrived in Paris on assignment in 1922. Three years later Flanner began crafting her famous column on French politics, art, theater, culture, and famous personalities of the time. She became a member of the expat literary community, attending the salons of Gertrude Stein and Natalie Barney. Flanner also befriended Hemingway—with whom she shared the personal tragedy of having a father who committed suicide. In her nearly fifty years on the job Flanner took her writing very seriously, believing that "genius is immediate, but talent takes time." Once back home she criticized her adopted country for being set in its ways: "France is a very old, civilized and impossible country." The French, on the other hand, appreciated Flanner and bestowed on her their highest decoration, the Légion d'honneur, in 1948.

Addresses for Flanner

- Hôtel Saint Germain at 36, rue Bonaparte (6ᵗʰ)—Flanner spent sixteen years living on the fourth floor of this hotel, still in operation today

- Les Deux Magots, 6, place Saint-Germain-des-Prés (6th)—Flanner and Solano often had breakfast at this café which they considered more sophisticated than those in Montparnasse; Flanner and Hemingway had serious discussions at a table in the back

- La Quatrième République, 42, rue Jacob (6th)—Flanner and Solano often dined at a small restaurant formerly found at this address

- The Living Room, then located at 25, rue du Colisée (8th)—the couple sometimes frequented this one-time jazz bar

- Hôtel Continental (now the Westin Paris), 3, rue de Castiglione (1st)—for two decades Flanner had a room on this hotel's top floor with a view of the Tuileries; she often "held court" in the hotel bar as well

- Hôtel Ritz, 15, place Vendôme (1st)—before returning definitively to New York in 1975 Flanner lived just above the tree line in this luxury hotel

A. J. Liebling (1904-1963)

No doubt about it: Liebling loved all things French, especially his culinary experiences in the *ville gastronomique*. He spells it out in his delightful memoir, *Between Meals: An Appetite for Paris*. Liebling first got to know the French capital as the son of a Manhattan furrier who often brought the family to Europe. After getting a degree in journalism at Columbia, the young man wrote first for a newspaper in Providence, Rhode Island and then for *The New York Times*. When these jobs didn't pan out to his liking, he fabricated a story about wanting to marry an older woman to get his father to pay for him to study at the Sorbonne. Instead of focusing on classes, however, Liebling studied the *Guide du Gourmand à Paris* to find the best places in the city for food and drink. At the outset of World War II he was back in town, temporarily replacing Janet Flanner as the author of *Letter from Paris*. Liebling was terribly disappointed with the decline of the Parisian restaurant scene. He felt the main damage was caused by the *Guide Michelin*'s subordination of "art to business." In his writing Liebling was not a one-trick pony. He was also celebrated for his war reporting which secured for him the French Légion d'honneur.

Addresses for Liebling

- Hôtel Montaigne, 6, avenue Montaigne (then the Hôtel Théâtre Champs-Élysées)—Liebling spent just a week at this location in 1926 before realizing it was too steep for his budget

- Hôtel Saint Pierre, 4, rue de l'École-de-Médecine (5th)—he then moved on to this hotel which was more within his means

- Crédit Lyonnais, 19, boulevard des Italiens (2nd)—Liebling walked to this beautiful bank building each month to collect funds sent by his father

- Restaurant des Beaux-Arts, once located at 11 bis, rue Bonaparte (6th)—he frequented this restaurant where he especially enjoyed a glass of Tavel rosé

- Café Soufflet, formerly at 25, boulevard Saint-Michel (5th)—this former café matched the image Liebling found in stories by Guy de Maupassant

- Pet places still in operation include: Benoît, 20, rue Saint-Martin, where Liebling enjoyed the weekly *pot-au-feu* beef stew (4th); Drouant, for its famous oysters, 18-16, rue Gaillon (2nd); and the Closerie des Lilas, 171, boulevard du Montparnasse (6th) where he celebrated at the liberation of Paris in August 1944

- Hôtel Louvois, 58, rue de Richelieu (2nd)—Liebling spent nearly nine months during World War II at this former hotel across from the old Bibliothèque Nationale

- Gypsy formerly at 20, rue Cujas (5th)—he enjoyed this bar which he found more French than those along the boulevard Montparnasse

Dorothy Parker (1893-1967)

As a girl in West End, New Jersey, Dorothy Rothschild was said to be "a plain disagreeable child…with a yen to write poetry." What's that saying about a zebra not changing its stripes? Years later, at New York's Algonquin Hotel Round Table she was quite clever but often mean-spirited. Her career began in earnest when, out of dire necessity, she sent poems to *Vogue* magazine. The job she got there in 1914—writing captions under pictures for ten dollars a week—was sufficient for her needs but far from ideal. That same year she began a fourteen-year marriage to stockbroker Edwin Parker, joking that she was just after "a nice, clean name." Dottie contributed articles to several magazines and became the drama critic for *Vanity Fair*. At the Round Table lunches Parker helped create, she met Ernest Hemingway and decided to go to Paris to become "a real writer." In February 1926, she arrived for an eight-month stay in the City of Light, describing it as "la belle, la brave, la raw, la rainy." With her limited French, Parker felt isolated and quipped that her listeners needed to be "reasonably adept at pantomime." Still, she was delighted to rub elbows with other members of the literary expatriate community which included Hemingway as well as Scott Fitzgerald and Archie MacLeish.

Addresses for Parker

- Hôtel Lutetia, 45 boulevard Raspail (6th)—luxury hotel where Parker stayed on her first trip to Paris from late February to early November 1926

- Closerie des Lilas (171, boulevard du Montparnasse) and the Dingo Bar (10, rue Delambre), now called Auberge de Venise, in Montparnasse (6th and 14th), and Bricktop's (once found at 66, rue Jean-Baptiste Pigalle) in Montmartre (18th)—bars and a cabaret she frequented with writer friends such as Hemingway and Fitzgerald

- Hôtel Napoléon, 40, avenue de Friedland (8th)—Parker took a room at this hotel near the Arc de Triomphe on a trip in 1929

- Hôtel Le Meurice at 228, rue de Rivoli (1ˢᵗ)—she and future husband actor Alan Campbell stayed here in the summer of 1933

- Hôtel de Crillon, 10, place de la Concorde (8ᵗʰ)—the couple enjoyed drinks with Janet Flanner at this lavish hotel's bar

- Brasserie Lipp, 151, boulevard Saint-Germain (6ᵗʰ)—a favorite dining spot for Parker

George Plimpton (1927-2003)

The "best-loved man in New York," according to author Norman Mailer, was an affable, witty, and urbane journalist and editor. "To the manor born" in Manhattan, Plimpton's ancestors arrived on the Mayflower. An Exeter and Harvard grad, he was studying at Cambridge when his boyhood friend Peter Matthiessen asked him to come to Paris to discuss establishing a literary magazine. After moving to the French capital, Plimpton first lived in the toolshed behind the house of Gertrude Stein's nephew Allan. He then relocated to not-much-better quarters: a cot on a small barge in the Seine which became the "headquarters" of *The Paris Review*. Because his roommate, future bandleader Peter Duchin, was a music student at the Sorbonne, the boat was outfitted with a piano but only had a pot-bellied stove for heat and no running water. He and roommates Duchin and Bob Silvers, future editor *The New York Review of Books*, supposedly shaved with Perrier. The lavish Hôtel Plaza Athénée just up the street unknowingly provided the fledgling journal with stationery. Plimpton worked hard at editing during the day but relaxed at jazz clubs or the bars of ritzy hotels at night. In Paris of the 1950s Plimpton believed you could get into any level of society "so long as you had a black tie and evening clothes."

Addresses for Plimpton

- Pont d'Alma, near the Alma-Marceau métro stop (8ᵗʰ)—Plimpton lived on a barge in the Seine moored near this bridge; the army cot he slept on was too short for his 6'4" frame

- Hôtel Plaza Athénée, 25, avenue Montaigne (8th)—Plimpton "borrowed" stationery from the lobby of this chic hotel, a short walk from the boat, to write letters for *The Paris Review*

- Éditions de la Table Ronde, 8, rue Garancière (6th)—the first non-floating office for the journal was a tiny room at this publishing house

- Le Tournon, 18, rue Tournon (6th)—the staff would often meet at this café just around the corner from their office on the rue Garancière to do their work and play pinball

- 16, rue Vernet (8th)—the workplace was eventually relocated to this address off the Champs-Élysées

- Hôtel Ritz, 15, place Vendôme (1st)—where Plimpton dropped by for drinks; he also spoke to Hemingway here and arranged an interview after seeing the author buy a copy of *The Paris Review*

- Hôtel de Crillon, 10, place de la Concorde (8th)—he loved relaxing at this luxury hotel bar after work

David Sedaris (1956-)

Time magazine's 2001 humorist of the year, Sedaris is best known for *Me Talk Pretty One Day*, essays dealing in part with his fractured French. Other fodder for his writing came from his dysfunctional family as well as a series of unusual jobs—including work as a field laborer in California and an elf in Macy's at Christmastime. Since the late 1990s, Sedaris and his partner Hugh Hamrick have maintained homes in Europe. Their Left Bank residence was coincidentally the original site of Sylvia Beach's Shakespeare and Company. Ironically, although he moved to the City of Light to learn French, he avoided speaking the language as much as possible. His reluctance to communicate was not helped at all by a Parisian teacher who told him "Every day spent with you is like having a Caesarian section." Still, Sedaris remained charmed by the city's beauty even after a decade living there. Perhaps fueled by the comedic tradition, he was far from an ordinary sightseer—never setting foot in Notre-Dame or the

Louvre. Likewise, when people visited, Sedaris enjoyed taking them to unusual sights such as puppet shows at the Luxembourg Gardens or the unique all-frozen-food store Picard. His favorite things included going to American movies, an auction house, or flea markets, where he presumably had to unearth at least a few words of French.

Addresses for Sedaris

- 8, rue Dupuytren (6th)—Sedaris's apartment on the Left Bank, the original home of Sylvia Beach's Shakespeare and Company
- 6, avenue Princesse (6th)—at times he enjoyed stopping in for readings at the Village Voice Bookshop off the rue du Four
- Drouot, 9, rue Drouot (9th)—Sedaris sometimes took visitors to this large auction house which features fine art and antiques
- Picard, 6, rue du 4 septembre (2nd)—one of the many locations of the frozen food chain in the capital

Susan Sontag (1933-2004)

A highly regarded novelist, essayist, and activist, Sontag won the National Book Award and a MacArthur Foundation "genius award." But more than a serious intellectual she was a complex, vulnerable person who appreciated cheesy movies and even posed for a photo in a teddy bear suit. Born Susan Rosenblatt in New York City, she assumed the name Sontag from her stepfather. While in college at Berkeley, the young woman became romantically involved with future writer Harriet Sohmers. Two years later Sontag married University of Chicago professor Philip Rieff who then took a teaching job in Boston. Sontag attended Harvard and won a scholarship to Oxford. But when she learned that Sohmers was in Paris, she decided to study at the Sorbonne instead. A few years following her divorce from Rieff, she and their son began living in the French capital full time in the late 1960s. For a while Sontag was infatuated with the culture of France though she later regarded it as extremely misogynistic. She moved back to the U.S. in the mid-70s after being diagnosed with cancer.

Sontag spent the last fifteen years of her life with photographer Annie Leibovitz who shot her picture on the *quai* near their home in Paris as well as at her desk wearing the famous bear suit.

Addresses for Sontag

- Grand Hôtel de l'Univers, 6, rue Grégoire de Tours (6th), now a Best Western—Sontag and Sohmers spent ten days at this hotel

- 31, rue de la Faisanderie (16th)—Sontag lived for a while at the garden pavilion home of her one-time lover Nicole Stéphane, a Rothschild heiress

- 42, rue Bonaparte (6th)—she spent a few months at this former apartment of author Jean-Paul Sartre in 1971

- 2, rue Séguier (6th)—Sontag and Leibovitz's apartment just off the quai des Grands Augustins 3, boulevard Edgar Quinet (14th)— address of the Montparnasse cemetery where Sontag's grave is found in section 2; getting a map at the entrance will help you find your way

Chapter 8

Politicians

ALTHOUGH THE UNITED STATES and France have had their political differences over the years (remember the whole "freedom fries" episode at the beginning of the war in Iraq?), close ties were established early in our country's history. In fact, even before our independence from Great Britain, the young Marquis de Lafayette came to our shores to volunteer his services—free of charge, mind you—in the American Revolution. The French government then supplied soldiers, sailors, and arms which vitally aided our emerging nation in winning the war, gaining its freedom, and getting on its feet. Ben Franklin and Thomas Jefferson, who each held the title of Minister Plenipotentiary in the late eighteenth century, were the first to represent the United States in an official capacity in Paris. Subsequently, an array of diplomats and politicians, such as John Adams, John Quincy Adams, James Monroe, and Thomas Paine, took up residence in the French capital. The following extremely abbreviated list of American statesmen includes Mitt Romney, who, although he was not a politician during his youth in France, would obviously go on to hold elected office decades later.

John Adams (1735-1826)

A strongly principled and very opinionated man, Adams was "absolutely out of his senses" at times, according to Ben Franklin. But

Adams was no doubt a leader who got things done. He served on the committee to draft the Declaration of Independence and went on to become our country's second president. His first trip to Paris in 1778 was to help Franklin secure aid from the French during the Revolutionary War. Four years later Adams was back in the city with Franklin and John Jay to arrange for peace negotiations. Thomas Jefferson, for one, was worried about how the brash Adams would conduct himself given that "He hates Franklin, he hates John Jay, he hates the French, he hates the English." Obviously, things worked out and the Treaty of Paris was signed in early September 1783. Besides his frequently uncompromising ways, Adams spoke no French and was not very interested in European culture. He was not unaware of the appeal of the French capital, however; in letters home to his wife Abigail he wrote of the "charming" gardens and "exquisite" statues in both the Palais Royal and the Tuileries. In 1784 he and his family took up residence outside the city limits in Auteuil. From there, Adams often took the one-mile walk to Franklin's home in Passy where the two statesmen met at times with Jefferson.

Addresses for Adams

- Hôtel de Valois, once located at 17, rue de Richelieu (1st)—with his ten-year-old son (and future president) Johnny, Adams first stayed in this hotel during a 1778 trip to secure financial and military aid from the French

- Hôtel de Valentinois, 64-72, rue Raynouard (16th)—father and son then moved in with Ben Franklin at his home at this address in Passy

- Hôtel Jacob (now the Hôtel d'Angleterre), 44, rue Jacob (6th)—at this location, formerly the British Embassy, Adams, Franklin, and John Jay drafted the Treaty of Paris, which brought an end to the American Revolution

- Hôtel d'York, 56, rue Jacob (6th)—the peace treaty was then signed at this address giving the United States full recognition as a country;

a white plaque marks this important event in American history

- Hôtel de Verrières, 43-47, rue d'Auteuil (16th)—Jefferson frequently visited Adams and his family at this large residence they rented outside of town to escape "the putrid streets of Paris" in 1784-85; another historical plaque is located here as well

John Quincy Adams (1767-1848)

At his boyhood home in Massachusetts he was called Johnny and later as JQA to distinguish him from his diplomat father. The second of five children, the young boy was a prodigy who became a great scholar and translator. And JQA was no slouch in the political field either: serving variously as a diplomat, a cabinet minister, the 6th president of the United States, and finally seventeen years in the House of Representatives. Much of his youth was spent abroad, including several sojourns in France. Beginning in April 1778 the ten year old accompanied his father on a political assignment in Paris. The boy studied languages at Le Cœur pension in Passy—quickly surpassing his father's knowledge of French. He was charmed by Parisian culture but assured his mother in letters home that he hoped not to be tempted by the "vice and folly" surrounding him. His time abroad was probably a contributing factor to his aristocratic manners as an adult; for sure, it is where he began a lifelong love of the theatre. Back in the French capital in 1815, the often-busy public servant was able to enjoy "three months of leisure" with fine dinners and trips to the Louvre, the opera, libraries, and bookstalls of the bouquinistes.

Addresses for John Quincy Adams

- Hôtel de Valois, no longer at 17, rue de Richelieu (1st) and Franklin's home at 64-72, rue Raynouard (16th)—two locations where the young boy stayed with his father in 1778

- Hôtel de Verrières, 43-47, rue d'Auteuil (16th)—JQA lived in this spacious house with the family from 1784 to 1785

- Hôtel du Nord, 97, rue de Richelieu (2ⁿᵈ)—beginning in February 1815, Adams spent three months at this one-time hotel, now the Passage des Princes; his wife Louisa and son Charles joined him in March

Benjamin Franklin (1706-1790)

Was there anything Ben Franklin couldn't do? Well, he never got his chance to be president, but just the same he had quite a long list of accomplishments: author, publisher, scientist, inventor, Founding Father, and the eighteenth-century equivalent of ambassador to France. After growing up in Boston, he lived in Philadelphia and London where he made important scientific discoveries—such as the lightning rod and the Gulf Stream—and issued his yearly *Poor Richard's Almanack* for over twenty-five years. As a member of the Committee of Five in June 1776, Franklin helped draft the Declaration of Independence. Six months later as the first Minister Plenipotentiary to France he helped to secure financial and military support from the French for the American Revolution. An important document Franklin worked on in 1782-83 was the Treaty of Paris which ended the war and established the United States as an independent country. During his nine years in the French capital, the amusing intellectual was greatly admired by French politicians and scientists. Even past age seventy, he was adored by Parisian women who kissed and flirted with him, sat on his lap, and called him Daddy Dear, *Cher Papa*. The French still love Franklin as evidenced by a bronze statue in the Square de Yorktown near the Palais de Chaillot and art devoted to him in the Petit Palais museum and the Procope café.

Addresses for Franklin

- Hôtel d'Entragues, 2-4, rue de l'Université (7ᵗʰ)—in December 1776 Franklin spent a few weeks at this former hotel, followed by several months at the Hôtel de Hambourg, once located at 52, rue Jacob (6ᵗʰ)

- Hôtel de Valentinois, 64-72 rue Raynouard (16ᵗʰ)—in 1777, at the invitation of Jacques-Donatien le Ray de Chaumont, called the "French father of the American Revolution," Franklin moved into part of his home in Passy; a plaque here commemorates Franklin and his installation of the first lightning rod in France.

- Le Procope, 13, rue de l'Ancienne Comédie (6th)—the oldest café in Paris was famous for clients such as Voltaire and Robespierre as well as Franklin who prepared the Treaty of Alliance here; inside, look for his bust and a bronze plaque with his name

- Hôtel de Coislin at 4, place de la Concorde and next door at the Hôtel de Crillon, 10, place de la Concorde (8th)—locations where Franklin signed the Treaty of Alliance, for military support, and the Treaty of Amity and Commerce, a commercial agreement, in 1778; look for the historical plaque on the Hôtel de Coislin at the corner of rue Royale

- Hôtel d'Angleterre (then called the Hôtel Jacob), 44, rue Jacob, and the former Hôtel d'York at 56, rue Jacob (6th)—where John Adams, John Jay, and Franklin prepared and then on September 3, 1783 signed the Treaty of Paris ending the American Revolutionary War; a white historical plaque on the Hôtel d'York marks this important event in our history

- Square de Yorktown, 1, avenue Paul Doumer (16th)—small park near the Trocadéro métro station (just to the west of the Palais de Chaillot) where a bronze statue of Franklin can be found

- Le Petit Palais, avenue Winston Churchill (8th)—art devoted to Franklin is located inside this free museum

Thomas Jefferson (1743-1826)

This Founding Father was a busy man: the principal author of the Declaration of Independence, a governor in his home state of Virginia, and, of course, the third president of the U.S. Before the presidency, however, Jefferson became depressed at the death of his young wife. Several friends, including John Adams, encouraged him to spend some time abroad. A few years later Jefferson took their advice and sailed to France in 1784. He was immediately taken with the capital: "A walk about Paris will provide lessons in history, beauty, and in the point of life." Once Ben Franklin left for home in 1785, Jefferson succeeded him as Minister Plenipotentiary and spent four more years enjoying the cuisine, wine, arts, and social life of Paris. The architecture of the city didn't escape his notice, either. In fact, he was so "violently smitten" with the Hôtel de Salm, under construction on the Left Bank at the time, that he would visit the Tuileries Garden almost every day to gaze at it across the Seine. He ultimately decided to redo the dome of his home in Monticello in the image of the mansion. A 2006 statue depicts Jefferson standing near the Seine, looking towards his favorite building with the plans for his Virginia residence in his hands.

Addresses for Jefferson

- Hôtel d'Orléans, 30, rue Richelieu (2nd)—Jefferson first stayed at this address, which has been replaced, before moving on to another former hotel coincidentally of the same name at 17, rue Bonaparte, then called the rue des Petits-Augustins (6th)

- Hôtel Landron, 5, Cul-de-Sac Taitbout, the present-day rue du Helder (9th)—this building, where he spent one year, has also been changed

- Hôtel de Langeac, 92, avenue des Champs-Élysées at the corner of Berri (8th)—Jefferson eventually settled into a twenty-four room mansion he would renovate at this address; a white historical plaque indicates the location of the original residence

- Le Procope, 13, rue de l'Ancienne Comédie (6th)—like Franklin, Jefferson also patronized this café, still open for business today

- Hôtel de Salm, 64, rue de Lille (7th)—Jefferson fell in love with this building's design and revamped the dome of his home at Monticello to look like it

- Statue of Jefferson, quai Anatole France at the foot of the Passerelle Léopold Sédar Senghor (7th)—near the Musée d'Orsay one finds an impressive sculpture of Jefferson looking at the Hôtel de Salm with plans for Monticello in his left hand

- Square Thomas-Jefferson, 1, place des États-Unis (16th)—here you find a bust and plaques dedicated to our third president as well as to the memory of those killed in the 2001 terrorist attacks in the U.S.

James Monroe (1758-1831)

The so-called "last Founding Father" was just a teenager when he fought as a soldier in the Continental Army. Monroe then went on to study law and become a U.S. senator. In August 1794 he took his wife and 8-year-old daughter to Paris where he began his tenure as Minister to France. A few months after arriving, Monroe gave a warm speech to the French legislative body which discussed both countries' shared belief in the "equal and unalienable rights of men." The French were delighted but not so much the Federalists back home who felt he showed favor to France over England. Monroe was relieved of his duties a mere two years later, but during his time at the post he succeeded in getting Tom Paine and other American prisoners released from French prison. In April 1803 President Jefferson sent Monroe back to the French capital to help negotiate the Louisiana Purchase. Up to the challenge, Monroe took advantage of France being strapped for cash during the Napoleonic Wars and bought the huge tract of land for just three cents an acre. Like Jefferson before him, Monroe was a big fan of the city's culture and lifestyle. Books, Parisian recipes, and other "souvenirs" like Louis XVI furniture eventually showed up at the White House when Monroe became our country's fifth president.

Addresses for Monroe

- Hôtel Cusset, 95, rue de Richelieu (2nd)—the home of the previous American Minister, Monroe lived here temporarily with his family and freed prisoner Thomas Paine; its old name can be seen engraved above the door

- 24, rue de Vintimille (9th)—in early 1796 Monroe bought an elegant, "jewel-like" mansion called La Folie de la Bouëxière in Montmartre to serve as the diplomatic residence; the house, which soon changed its main entrance to 6, rue de Clichy, was demolished in 1840

Thomas Paine (1737-1809)

Paine's mundane life in his native England included work as a rope maker, customs officer, and schoolteacher. How then, one might ask, did he come to be considered the "Father of the American Revolution"? It all started when a friend in London introduced Paine to Ben Franklin in 1774. Because Franklin thought the young man might make a good clerk or surveyor in Philadelphia, he helped Paine emigrate to the colonies. Paine took a job as a journalist at a magazine and two years later published his forty-eight page work *Common Sense*. The widely-read pamphlet helped energize insurgents and led Founding Fathers to reject plans for a British form of government. But Paine wasn't done traveling or involving himself in uprisings. Because of the growing conflicts in the French Revolution, he moved to Paris in the 1790s. Quite surprisingly, he was elected a member of France's National Assembly despite the fact that he couldn't speak any French. However, his fortune changed dramatically when he took the unpopular position of being opposed to the execution of King Louis XVI. Paine was then thrown into prison—only to escape the guillotine through the efforts of American Minister (and future president) James Monroe.

Addresses for Paine

- Hôtel White, 1, rue des Petits Pères (2nd)—Paine stayed briefly at this former hotel near the Galerie Vivienne before moving nearby to 7, Passage des Petits Pères (2nd); neither building nor address still exists

- 144, rue du Faubourg Saint-Denis (10th)—he rented a former farmhouse with six others at this address in 1793

- Palais du Luxembourg, 17, rue du Vaugirard (6th)—now home to the French Senate, the former palace was a prison during the Reign of Terror; Paine was jailed there for treason at the end of 1793 for nearly a year

- Hôtel Cusset, 95, rue de Richelieu (2nd) and 24, rue de Vintimille (9th)—weak from his imprisonment and lacking resources, Paine lived for nearly two years with future president James Monroe and his family at these addresses; the old name of the Hôtel Cusset can still be seen engraved above the door

- 10, rue de l'Odéon (6th)—from 1797 till 1802, Paine resided at this Left Bank address, now marked with a white plaque

Mitt Romney (1947-)

This political figure's name will be quite familiar to most readers since he served as Massachusetts governor and ran as a 2012 presidential candidate. What may be new is that he spent nearly three years in France as a Mormon missionary which he once characterized as an "enriching" time. Born in Detroit, he is the son of another well-known Republican politician George Romney. After a year at Stanford, Mitt and eight other young missionaries took a flight from Utah to the French capital in July 1966. Once in Le Havre, their home base, Romney and the others had the unenviable task of trying to convert French people to their faith. Adding to their difficulty, they were required to go door-to-door on bikes for up to ten hours a day. At the beginning of the following year, Romney lived in southwest France until being transferred to Paris in May. According to his roommate Dr. Mulloy Hansen, their fourth-floor walk-up in Montparnasse was "the worst place to live among the many apartments in the mission." Besides sharing squat toilet facilities with two other apartments, they had to rig up a shower with a hose and a small, plastic tub in the kitchen. In 1968 Romney had slightly better quarters in an attic room of the elegant mission house in the 16th arrondissement. His time abroad was marked by a tragic car accident near Bordeaux which severely injured him and took the life of the mission leader's wife.

Addresses for Romney

- 126, rue du Château (14th)—beginning in May 1967 Romney shared an apartment in this building not far from the Montparnasse train station

- 3, rue de Lota (16th)—site of the magnificent mission house where he lived under the eaves in 1968

Chapter 9

Artists and Architects

THE FRENCH CAPITAL HAS long been considered a center for the visual arts. As early as the Middle Ages, monarchs began collecting precious relics while on Crusades in the Holy Land. Renaissance king François I, impressed by Italian art in the sixteenth century, not only brought the *Mona Lisa* to Paris but its painter Leonardo da Vinci as well. (Maybe you were wondering how that painting found its way to the Louvre!) Besides the impressive holdings in museums and galleries, the city itself had undergone reconstruction by the prefect Baron Haussmann in the mid-nineteenth century. The destruction of 12,000 structures—some of historical import— had been quite controversial at the time. Haussmann did, however, manage to transform the once-dingy capital into the beautiful city we so admire today, by establishing impressive, homogeneous architecture, wide avenues, and large parks. Around this time painters, sculptors, photographers, and architects began flocking to Paris. Some came to study with a particular teacher or to attend classes at the prestigious fine arts school, l'École des Beaux-Arts. Many were able to share ideas with a long list of international artists thanks to the vibrant café life. This chapter concentrates on eleven prominent Americans from the art world: architects such as Richard Morris Hunt and Henry Hobson Richardson and Impressionist artist Mary Cassatt in the mid-eighteen-hundreds, and sculptor

Alexander Calder in the 1920s, among others.

Alexander Calder (1898-1976)

If you've ever seen a *mobile*, you probably already know the works of "Sandy" Calder. His career in the arts started off early when, as a child in Philadelphia, he fashioned jewelry out of beads and wire for his sister's dolls. His degree in mechanical engineering, believe it or not, would come in handy later on when he decided to focus on the arts. While working as an illustrator for the *National Police Gazette*, he was sent to observe the Ringling Brothers Circus—which would play a big part in future creations. Calder moved to Paris in July 1926 and fell so in love with the city that he ended up staying seven years. After all, the avant-garde center was perfect for him: beautiful art and architecture with an impressive array of international artists including Piet Mondrian, Joan Miró, Alberto Giacometti, and Fernand Léger. In fact, two of his friends, Marcel Duchamp and Jean Arp, were responsible for naming Calder's innovations: mobiles for moving sculptures and stabiles for stationary objects. When a Serbian toy merchant suggested that he try his hand at making jointed toys, Calder recalled visiting Ringling Brothers and fashioned a miniature wire circus, complete with performers, animals, and props. He performed his Cirque Calder to audiences from Paris to New York.

Addresses for Calder

- Hôtel de Versailles, 60, boulevard du Montparnasse (6th)—Calder spent his first month with a friend's father at this location, no longer a hotel

- Hôtel Le Lionceau at 22, rue Daguerre (14th)—he then took a small room at this Montparnasse hotel, still in business

- Académie de la Grande Chaumière at 14, rue de la Grande Chaumière (6th)—Calder took drawing classes at this school, also still in operation

- 7, rue Cels (14th)—for about six months the artist lived in this building around the corner from the rue Daguerre
- Le Dôme, 108, boulevard du Montparnasse (14th)—Calder's routine in Paris consisted of working until early afternoon followed by discussions with fellow artists at this café
- 7, Villa Brune (14th)— in January 1931 after marrying Louisa James, grandniece of author Henry James, Calder and his bride lived at this address on a quiet cul-de-sac
- 14, rue de la Colonie (13th)—a few months later, the couple moved to the top floor of a three-story house which no longer exists

Mary Cassatt (1844-1926)

Bold, independent women come from Allegheny, Pennsylvania—if Gertrude Stein and Mary Cassatt are typical examples. Like Stein, thirty years her junior, Cassatt came from an affluent family but found her true home in France. She asserted that in Paris "Women do not have to fight for recognition…if they do serious work." As a youth, Cassatt was bored with typical homemaking classes designed for women of her time and took the audacious step of enrolling at the Pennsylvania Academy of Fine Arts. Frustrated by condescending attitudes of teachers and students as well as the lack of courses, she decided to study art in Europe. Against her father's objections to living a "bohemian life" abroad, she moved to Paris in 1866 and took private lessons at the Louvre. Two years later one of her paintings was selected for the prestigious Paris Salon, an honor which was repeated several times and secured her reputation. Cassatt's works, which focus primarily on the daily life of women and children, surprised fellow artist Edgar Degas who thought women only painted as if they were "trimming hats." His invitation for her to participate in an Impressionist exhibition began their forty-year friendship. Cassatt became a lifelong French resident, eventually purchasing the Château de Beaufresne, about an hour's drive north of Paris, in the town of Le Mesnil-Théribus where she is buried.

Addresses for Cassatt

- 19, rue de Laval, now rue Victor Massé (9th)—in 1874 Cassatt and her sister Lydia spent two years in a studio in Montmartre

- 13, avenue Trudaine (9th)—when their parents came to live with the two young women, the family spent a few months on the rue Beaujon near the Arc de Triomphe (8th) before moving to a top-story apartment at this address in the 9th

- 10, rue de Marignan (8th)—in 1887 the Cassatts lived near the Champs-Élysées; a white historical plaque marks the building

Richard Morris Hunt (1827-1895)

"The Father of American Architecture" is well known and for good reason. He created the façade of the New York Metropolitan Museum of Art, the Breakers mansion in Newport, Rhode Island, and the Biltmore Estate in Asheville, North Carolina. Not a bad abbreviated résumé. Hunt listened to his clients' wishes but was undoubtedly stretching the point when he said: "If they want you to build a house upside down standing on its chimney, it's up to you to do it." A native of Brattleboro, Vermont, he first went to Europe with his mother and brothers after his father's untimely death. For a while Hunt was enrolled in a military academy in Geneva which he hated. On the positive side, though, it provided him with an introduction to architecture. Encouraged by his family, Hunt attended Paris's École des Beaux-Arts, the premier architectural school in the world. He spent nine happy years in the French capital studying but also getting practical experience working on projects like renovations at the Louvre. Witnessing the Haussmannian transformation of Paris possibly inspired Hunt to become part of the City Beautiful Movement back home. In 1882 the French protector of the arts, the Institut de France, made him an associate member of their Fine Arts Academy, an honor rarely bestowed upon a foreign national.

Addresses for Hunt

- École nationale supérieure des Beaux-Arts, 14, rue Bonaparte (6th)—The first American to study architecture at this prestigious fine arts school, Hunt was awarded its highest student prize: the Grand Prix de Rome

- 1, rue Jacob (6th)—he and his brother William, an art student, shared an apartment near the school and just down the street from their mother's place at number 23

- 21, avenue des Champs-Élysées (8th)—during their 1½–year honeymoon, Hunt and his wife lived part of their time at this address where their first child was born

- Hôtel Continental (now the Westin Paris), 3, rue de Castiglione (1st)—just two years before his death, Hunt was back in Paris with his wife and stayed at this hotel

Charles Follen McKim (1847-1909)

When it comes to impressive designs, this architect was no slacker. He designed the Boston Public Library, Manhattan's original Penn Station, and the Isaac Bell House in Newport, Rhode Island, to name a few. Born in Chester County, Pennsylvania, Charlie spent a disappointing year in engineering classes at Harvard. Because he loved to draw, in 1867 he decided to join his college friend Robert Peabody who was going to Paris to study architecture. McKim's father was not too enthralled with his son studying in Paris, but the idea of a prestigious European education helped him relent. The two young men joined a third Harvard man Francis Chandler and spent three years in the city living, studying, and traveling together. McKim enjoyed the dazzling architecture as well as the street life of the French capital. An athlete, he encouraged his friends to work out no matter what the season. They threw around a baseball in the Luxembourg Gardens near their apartment in warm weather and went ice skating in the Bois de Boulogne in winter. In July 1868 the three of them paddled an outrigger canoe up the Seine to Rouen—no small feat, given that the cities are seventy miles apart.

Addresses for McKim

- 1, rue de Fleurus (6th)—McKim, Peabody, and Chandler shared an apartment at this address opposite the Luxembourg Gardens

- 18, rue de l'Abbaye (6th)—all three young men enrolled at the atelier of Honoré Daumet before being accepted into architecture classes at the renowned École des Beaux-Arts, 14, rue Bonaparte (6th)

- Bibliothèque Sainte-Geneviève, 10, place du Panthéon (5th)—McKim later drew on the design of this building to complete the façade of the Boston Public Library in Copley Square

Samuel F. B. Morse (1791-1872)

You might be asking yourself: "Isn't that the Morse Code guy who invented the telegraph?" Well, yes, but Morse was a pretty clever fellow—both an inventor and an artist. A native of Charlestown, Massachusetts, he studied electricity at Yale before seriously disappointing his parents by turning to drawing and painting. A year after graduation, he convinced his folks to let him study art in London. He returned to the U.S. and earned a living as a portraitist and was even commissioned to do paintings of presidents John Adams and James Monroe. After his wife died, Morse entrusted his children to his brothers and, in 1830, moved to the French capital. He was eager to immerse himself in the Louvre, "the most splendid…collection of works of art in the world." Which is exactly what he did. Like other artists, Morse spent time copying museum masterpieces. Then, over a period of two years, he incorporated miniatures of thirty-eight of its works into his huge painting *The Gallery of the Louvre*. On the ship home in October 1832 he had discussions with an expert in electromagnetism which led to Morse's famous inventions. At age seventy-five, he and his family were back for a two-year stay in Paris. During this time he was awarded the Légion d'honneur for his discoveries by Emperor Napoleon III.

Addresses for Morse

- 29, rue de Surène (8th)—in 1830 he rented a small apartment on the Right Bank with his roommate, fellow painter Richard Habersham

- Hôtel du Louvre, which has been relocated to place André Malraux (1st)—on a return trip he stayed at this hotel

- L'Observatoire de Paris, 61, avenue de l'Observatoire (14th)—Morse demonstrated the telegraph at the Paris Observatory in 1838

- 10, avenue du Roi de Rome, the present-day avenue Kléber (16th)—late in life Morse and his family spent two years in this elegant apartment which took up the entire third floor

Man Ray (1890-1976)

This artist and photographer *extraordinaire* was all the rage in Paris for his photos. Many Americans including Djuna Barnes, Sinclair Lewis, and William Carlos Williams, rushed to his studio to sit for his natural, unposed pictures. And yes, Man Ray was his real name—sort of. He was born in Philadelphia to the Rudzitsky family who, because of antisemitism, simplified their last name to Ray. Young Emmanuel, called "Manny" as a child, shortened his first name to "Man" in adulthood. Ray spent several years as a painter in New York before leaving for the French capital in July 1921. His friend, French artist Marcel Duchamp, got him settled and introduced him to the founders of the Surrealist movement. For most of that decade Ray lived with artists' model Kiki de Montparnasse until beautiful American photographer Lee Miller caught his eye in his favorite café. She became his muse, protégée, and lover for three years. Ray spent the World War II years in Los Angeles where he married dancer/artists' model Juliet Browner. The couple moved to Paris in 1951, taking a cold, damp studio which had once been a garage. Their early days were "more like camping" but the artist continually worked at fixing the place up and lived there for the rest of his life.

Addresses for Ray

- Hôtel Boulainvilliers at 12, rue de Boulainvilliers (16th)—with Duchamp's help Ray got a room at this former hotel in Passy which had just been vacated by Surrealist poet Tristan Tzara

- 22, rue de la Condamine (17th)—Ray then spent four months in an attic room at this rather out-of-the-way site

- Grand Hôtel des Écoles 15, rue Delambre (14th)—he returned to the heart of the city, taking room #32 at this hotel, now known as the Lenox Montparnasse

- Hôtel Istria, 29, rue Campagne-Première (14th)—in the early 1920s Ray lived here with Alice Prin, aka Kiki of Montparnasse, the model for his celebrated *Le Violon d'Ingres* photo (see the historical plaque with his name); he also rented a ground-floor studio in the building next door at #31, bis

- 8, rue du Val-de-Grâce (5th)—in the mid-30s he had a studio at this address

- 2 bis, rue Férou (6th)—Ray lived at this location between Saint-Sulpice and the Luxembourg Gardens with his wife for the last twenty-five years of his life

- Cimetière du Montparnasse, 3, boulevard Edgar Quinet (14th)—Ray and his wife are buried in division 7, row 1 of this cemetery

Henry Hobson Richardson (1838-1886)

Fortunately for the architectural world, Richardson wasn't accepted to West Point and changed his major from civil engineering to architecture while at Harvard. After graduation Richardson took off for a tour of Britain and then spent five years in the City of Light. He wrote home to his fiancée: "Paris is to a man what college is to a boy…a dangerous place to send a young man"—not exactly reassuring for her, I'm sure. As a child in Louisiana, Richardson had learned French, which proved a great asset in fitting in with other students and getting admitted to the École des Beaux-Arts (the Fine Arts School). He studied at the atelier of Louis-Jules André and got practical and sometimes even paid experience working in architecture offices. That money, plus financial backing he received from home, allowed the young man to live, play, and dress extravagantly in the city…for a time at least. Once his family was ruined by the Civil War, however, Richardson was unable to finish his studies. This in no way put an end to his career. In fact, he became one of the most celebrated architects of the nineteenth century creating, among other buildings, Trinity Church in Boston, and both City Hall and the State House in Albany, New York.

Addresses for Richardson

- 41, rue de Vaugirard (15th)—Richardson first took a room in a pension at this address in 1859

- École des Beaux-Arts at 14, rue Bonaparte (6th)—he initially failed the entrance exam to study architecture at this world-renowned fine arts school, but got in the following year, placing 18th out of 120 applicants

- rue de Luxembourg, now called rue Cambon (1st); rue Mazarine (6th); the rue du Bac (7th)—various addresses (without numbers) where Richardson lived during his five years in Paris

Augustus Saint-Gaudens (1848-1907)

The leading American sculptor of the Gilded Age—designer of the Admiral Farragut statue in Manhattan and the Shaw Memorial in Boston—was actually born in Ireland. But since the potato famine sent him to the U.S. at six months of age, we get to claim him as our own. In his early teens, the red-haired boy showed an unmistakable knack for art. He apprenticed to a cameo-cutter and took drawing classes at Cooper Union. In February 1867, funded by his parents, the nineteen year old took off for Paris with plans to study sculpture. He first stayed with his Uncle François on the avenue de la Grande Armée behind the Arc de Triomphe. Saint-Gaudens remembered being "extraordinarily impressed" with the city and standing "bewildered" at the sight of the place de la Concorde and the Champs-Élysées. His cameo-cutting ability earned him a living on Montmartre while he took sculpting classes at a small school on the Left Bank. After a month or so, a teacher recommended the young man for classes at the famous École des Beaux-Arts where he spent three years…considerably more than the nine months he had originally planned. Saint-Gaudens was back in Paris with his wife in 1877. Mark Twain visited them at their apartment on the rue Herschel in the 6th arrondissement, as did painter John Singer Sargent.

Addresses for Saint-Gaudens

- 5, rue de l'École de Médicine (6th)—Saint-Gaudens took sculpture classes at the small École Royale Gratuite de Dessin once located at this address

- École des Beaux-Arts, 14, rue Bonaparte (6th)—he then became the first American to study sculpture at this renowned fine arts school from 1867-1870

- 178, boulevard Pereire (17th)—in 1877 he lived for a short while at this out-of-the-way location with his wife Gussie

- 3, rue Herschel (6th)—the couple then moved into larger premises on the fourth floor at this address off boulevard Saint-Michel near the Luxembourg Gardens

- 49, rue Notre-Dame des Champs (6th)—Saint-Gaudens had a very large studio at this former dance hall

John Singer Sargent (1856-1925)

Described by his friend Henry James as "civilized to his fingertips," Sargent apparently fit right in with the high-society crowd he painted. Extremely prolific, besides portraits over his career he dabbled in landscapes and the decorative arts, including a series of murals at the Boston Public Library. Sargent was born in Italy where his parents had moved after the death of a child in Philadelphia. To calm John's rambunctious behavior, his mother encouraged him to pursue art. He proved so adept at painting that the family moved to Paris in 1874 to advance their teenaged son's career. Sargent was devoted to his craft. His sister recalled him working "like a dog from morning till night" while studying with painter Carolus-Duran. After his portrait of wealthy American Madame Pierre Gautreau, termed *Madame X*, appeared in the 1884 Paris Salon, Sargent found himself at the center of a quite a commotion. The strap of the woman's black gown had, in the original, been "indecently" hanging off the woman's shoulder; the artist later altered the painting to restore the strap to its more decent place. Sargent's visit with Monet at Giverny initiated his Impressionist period, moving his easel outdoors. When he found it difficult to get commissions after the disgrace of the *Madame X* picture, Sargent moved to London where he spent most of the rest of his life.

Addresses for Sargent

- 52, rue de la Boétie (8th)—the Sargent family moved to this Right Bank location after leaving Italy in 1874

- 11, passage Stanislas, now the rue Jules Chaplain (6th)—address of Carolus-Duran's studio where Sargent studied painting and produced a famous portrait of his teacher

- École des Beaux-Arts at 14, rue Bonaparte (6th)—he was accepted into this fine arts school and began studying with portraitist Léon Bonnat

- 19, rue de l'Odéon (6th)—once he moved out of his parents' home, Sargent took a room at Madame Darode's boarding house at this address

- 73, rue Notre-Dame des Champs (6th)—he shared a fifth-floor art studio here with fellow American art student James Carroll Beckwith in 1875

- 81 and later 135, boulevard du Montparnasse (6th)—Sargent had two apartments along this boulevard; number 81 has since disappeared

- 41, boulevard Berthier (17th)—in the winter of 1883-1884 he moved to this address where he painted the controversial portrait of Madame X

Louis Sullivan (1856-1924)

Egotistical, impatient, and abrupt, Sullivan was nonetheless one of the most influential architects of the twentieth century. His axiom "form follows function" was just a starting point for his designs because he believed "the building's identity resided in the ornament." Sullivan spent one year at M.I.T.'s school of architecture then, following the advice of Richard Morris Hunt, apprenticed at firms in Philadelphia and Chicago. In 1874 he was finally able to realize his dream of living and studying in Paris. After being tutored in French and math, Sullivan entered the prominent École des Beaux-Arts. Although in letters home he complained about the "God damnedest kind of weather," Sullivan loved the "self-renewing youth" of the city and felt that the people had "the same light-hearted spirit of adventure" as Chicagoans. Sullivan saw it all: monuments, palaces, museums, and architectural exhibitions as well as the bars of Montparnasse. Yet, ever the restless student, he tired of traditional classes after six months and took off for Italy before returning home. Considered "the father of skyscrapers," Sullivan is acclaimed as the creator of important buildings in several U.S. cities. One of his great designs, Chicago's Carson Pirie Scott department store, has now been renamed The Sullivan Center in his honor.

Addresses for Sullivan

- École des Beaux-Arts, 14, rue Bonaparte (6th)—Sullivan passed the entrance exam and entered this famous school of fine arts

- 116, rue du Bac (7th)—he worked in the atelier of Émile Vaudremer, a short walk from the school

- 17, rue Racine (5th)—Sullivan had a small Left Bank apartment on the top floor of this building at the corner of rue Monsieur-le-Prince

James Whistler (1834-1903)

Arrangement in Gray and Black Number 1 may not ring a bell but becomes quite familiar under its popular name, *Whistler's Mother*. The portrait, the first American art work ever purchased by the French state, now hangs in Impressionist museum, the Musée d'Orsay. Whistler was like an adopted son in Paris since he lived and worked there for many years. The artist started life in Lowell, Massachusetts, but spent part of his childhood in St. Petersburg, Russia where he learned to speak Russian and French. Expelled from West Point after failing chemistry, Whistler decided to become an artist in the City of Light. Not a student of art, mind you: an artist. As a family friend once reported, the haughty Whistler "disdained taking lessons from anybody." For a while he shared a room in a small hotel on the rue Saint-Sulpice with his model/lover nicknamed Fumette until she angrily destroyed many of his drawings. A painting of a subsequent girlfriend in "The White Girl" was rejected from the Paris Salon in 1863 but received favorable notice at the Salon des Refusés, the "Exhibition of Rejects." After moving to London, Whistler found, for the most part, the critical acclaim he had been seeking in France. But four years later, having grown tired of the British capital, he returned to Paris, welcomed back by friends Monet and Rodin.

Addresses for Whistler

- École Impériale et Spéciale de Dessin, 5, rue de l'École de Médecine (5th)—Whistler studied for a short while at this school on the Left Bank

- 69, rue de Vaugirard (6th)—he then took classes from Swiss artist Charles Gleyre at his studio at this address

- Hôtel Corneille, 5, rue Corneille (6th)—Whistler lived at this former hotel along with many medical and art students

- 35, rue Jacob (6th)—he then moved to this location which was closer to the Louvre

- 1, rue Bourbon-le-Château (6th)—he took an apartment for a while near the boulevard Saint-Germain

- Café Corazza, 26, rue de Richelieu (1st)—Whistler met artists of the time, including Courbet and Fantin-Latour, at this café still in operation today

- 3, rue de Campagne-Première (14th)—location of Whistler's one-time atelier

- 110, rue du Bac (7th)—after four years in London, he moved back to Paris with his wife; a white historical plaque marks this apartment building

- 86, rue Notre-Dame des Champs (6th)—Whistler had a top-floor studio at this address

Chapter 10

Musicians and Performers

Just think of all the songs written about the French capital: "I Love Paris," "April in Paris," even "How Ya Gonna Keep 'Em Down on the Farm (After They've Seen Paree)"—and so many more. The city served as an inspiration, yes, but also as a home to many top people in the music field. Musicians and performers of every stripe from around the globe have been drawn to the city—some at the top of their art, others hoping for the big break which would lead to stardom. Americans, of course, are no exception; they have been heading to Paris in droves for over a century. There were modern dance pioneers, Loie Fuller and Isadora Duncan, who found fame and fortune (albeit fleeting in the second case) in the early 1900s. In the decades following the World Wars the city was inundated with a steady stream of prominent singers as different as banana-skirted performer Josephine Baker in the 1920s, jazz pianist and soloist Blossom Dearie in the 1950s, and "rock poet" Jim Morrison of The Doors two decades later. A variety of composers, too, uncovered the many artistic resources in the City of Light: Aaron Copland, Duke Ellington, George Gershwin, and Quincy Jones spring to mind. This chapter examines the lives and habitats of sixteen leaders in the world of dance and music who at one point in their lives chose to live and work in Paris.

Josephine Baker (1906-1975)

Against all odds, Freda Josephine McDonald would become the star of the Paris jazz scene. "The most sensational woman anyone ever saw," as Hemingway once described her, grew up in poverty in Saint Louis. Twice-married as teenager, she kept her second husband's name when she began touring the country as a dancer. At Harlem's Cotton Club, Baker gained notice for her clowning and improvising as well as admiration for her talents. On October 2, 1925 the nineteen year old premiered as the main attraction of the twenty-eight-member Revue Nègre in Paris and brought down the house. *La Vénus Noire*, The Black Venus, as she was called, later developed her landmark *Danse Sauvage* (Wild Dance) wearing a skirt of artificial bananas. Lovers were not lacking for Baker in the capital; they included a short, but torrid affair with Belgian mystery writer Georges Simenon, her secretary at the time. The director of a Parisian cabaret gifted her with a pet cheetah which she paraded around adorned with a diamond-studded leash, often scaring the daylights out of café patrons. Yet, La Baker was not just appreciated by the French for her performances. Her help in the Resistance Movement during World War II won her the military honor the Croix de guerre and France's highest award, the Légion d'honneur. Financially ruined toward the end of her life, Baker survived through the support of her friend and fellow American Princess Grace of Monaco.

Addresses for Baker

- Théâtre des Champs-Élysées, 15, avenue Montaigne (8th)—where the teenaged, nearly nude Baker opened to a full house with the smash hit Revue Nègre

- Hôtel Fournet, once located at 23, boulevard des Batignolles (8th)—the troupe of musicians and performers had rooms at this former hotel in Montmartre

- Folies Bergères, 32, rue Richer (9th)—in 1926 Baker first performed her famous banana skirt routine at this well-known music hall

- La Coupole 102, boulevard du Montparnasse (14th)—a mural of Baker can be found on a back right column of this café where she often came with lovers or her pet cheetah, Chiquita

- Chez Josephine, at 40, rue Pierre Fontaine (9th)—former address of Baker's own cabaret which served traditional French fare as well as soul food; it later relocated to 43, rue François 1er (8th)

- Casino de Paris, 16, rue de Clichy (9th)—in 1931 Baker's show at this music hall featured her theme song J'ai Deux Amours ("I Have Two Loves")…her two loves being her country and Paris

- 2, rue du Lieutenant Chauré (20th)—just before the outbreak of World War II, Baker spent several years in a lovely brick mansion in *le quartier de la Campagne* (the country quarter)

- Église de la Madeleine, place de la Madeleine (8th)—a state funeral was held for Baker at this prominent church in April 1975 before her burial in Monaco

Sidney Bechet (1897-1959)

The man Duke Ellington called "the very epitome of jazz" might not seem too familiar at first glance. But if you remember the recurring theme *"Si tu vois ma mère"* ("If You See My Mother") in Woody Allen's film *Midnight in Paris*, you know Bechet…or at least one of his tunes. A prodigy in his hometown of New Orleans, he started out playing his brother's clarinet at age six and later became a master of the soprano sax. Bechet never learned to read music but, with perfect pitch, could reproduce any song. In October 1925 as the star musician of *La Revue Nègre*, featuring Josephine Baker, he helped introduce African-American culture to Paris. Three years later he was back performing in the capital until a shootout with another musician outside Bricktop's cabaret landed him in jail for eleven months. Bechet was deported after his sentence was up but returned in 1949 to perform at Paris's International Festival de Jazz. An international celebrity at that point, he refused to play for segregated audiences, saying "If you like me, I want you to like my whole race." Bechet became a permanent resident of France in the early 1950s and bought a house in Garches, west of the capital, where he is buried.

Addresses for Bechet

- Théâtre de l'Apollo at 20, rue de Clichy (9th)—on his first trip to Paris in the summer of 1918 Bechet played with an orchestra at this former music hall

- Théâtre des Champs-Élysées at 15, avenue Montaigne (8th)—in 1925 he was the lead musician with the Revue Nègre starring Josephine Baker

- Ambassadeurs, 1-3, avenue Gabriel near the Champs-Élysées (8th), now called the Espace Pierre Cardin—Bechet performed here as a member of Noble Sisle's band in 1928

- 25, rue Hermel (18th)—that same year he wrote his brother from this address

- Chez Bricktop, once located at 66, rue Jean-Baptiste Pigalle (9th) and Chez Florence, 61, rue Blanche (9th)—two former clubs in Montmartre where Bechet used to play

- Salle Pleyel at 252, Faubourg Saint-Honoré (8th)—he was a hit at a jazz festival at this location in 1949 and decided to move permanently to France

- Hôtel Saint-Yves, 4, rue de l'Université (7th)—Bechet stayed at a hotel previously at this address in 1950

- Club du Vieux Colombier, 21, rue du Vieux Colombier (6th)—in 1956 Bechet and Lionel Hampton performed together in a small basement club formerly found here

Aaron Copland (1900-1990)

"The dean of American composers" dreamed big even as an eleven year old when he produced an opera for his family in Brooklyn. Later on, he gained renown for classic pieces such as "Fanfare for the Common

Man" and "Appalachian Spring." As a youth, Copland decided to concentrate on music instead of going to college and took classes with musician Rubin Goldmark. In June 1921 he headed for France to study at the newly formed American Conservatory at Fontainebleau, southeast of the city. In his first letter home, he told his parents that he was perplexed by Parisian menus and ate omelets several times in a row since it was the only French word he understood. Soon enough, though, the young man was enjoying "regular meals of the best kind for 75 cents" as well as finding his way to concerts, ballets, and museums. Early on in his studies, he met composer, conductor and professor, Nadia Boulanger, and recalled that "no one thought a woman could possibly hope to teach composition." But this particular woman impressed him so that she soon became his teacher, mentor, and greatest influence. In fact, Copland extended his stay in the country from one to three years to keep learning from "Mademoiselle Boulanger."

Addresses for Copland

- Hôtel Savoy, 30 rue de Vaugirard (6th)—when he first arrived in Paris in 1921, Copland took a room (for 70 cents a day!) at this one-time hotel where he had a comfortable bed but no running water

- 207, boulevard Raspail (14th)—in the fall of that year he and a distant relative (and future theatrical director), Harold Clurman rented a "crummy apartment" on the top floor of what is now a Mercure hotel

- 36, rue Ballu (9th)—Copland took classes from famed teacher Nadia Boulanger at Fontainebleau and later in her home at this address in the capital

- Villa d'Alésia, off the rue d'Alésia (14th)—the following year Copland and Clurman moved into much better quarters in the apartment of a singing instructor on this small cul-de-sac (no number given)

- 66, boulevard Pasteur (15th)—the roommates then took inexpensive rooms with a French family

Blossom Dearie (1924-2009)

"A genre unto herself" is how *The New York Times* once described this skillful jazz pianist with the distinctive, girlish voice. And that uniqueness extended right down to her name which Mr. and Mrs. Dearie conferred upon her after someone brought peach blossoms to their house the day she was born. A native of the Catskills in Upstate New York, she began piano lessons at age five and was accomplished at jazz improvisation as a teenager. After moving to Manhattan, Dearie performed with greats such as Dizzy Gillespie, Charlie Parker, and Woody Herman. In 1952 she was discovered at the Chantilly Club in Greenwich Village by Nicole Barclay, co-owner of a French recording label. Barclay then invite her to join the jazz scene in Paris. Dearie first shared living quarters with Scottish jazz singer Annie Ross and enjoyed the "easy hanging-out-in-cafés ambience of the capital." For five years she was quite successful with her octet the "Blue Stars" which scored a major hit with the French version of "Lullaby of Birdland." Dearie also met Belgian musician Bobby Jaspar who became her husband for a couple of years in the mid-1950s.

Addresses for Dearie

- Mars Club, 6, rue Robert Estienne (8th)—Dearie performed at this club now renamed Les Innocents near the Champs-Élysées

- Berlitz, 31, boulevard des Italiens (9th)—she took French classes at this former site of the famous language school

- The Living Room, once located at 25, rue du Colisée (8th)—Dearie and her friend Quincy Jones used to hang out at this jazz club

Isadora Duncan (1877-1927)

Considered the "Mother of Modern Dance" by many, Duncan made quite a splash in early twentieth-century Paris. In fact, *The New Yorker* columnist Janet Flanner called her "without question the most famous American" of the time. As a child Duncan studied ballet in

San Francisco and by age eighteen was a dancer with a New York City touring company. After moving to England with her mother and brother, the young woman immersed herself in the Greek artifacts at the British Museum as inspiration for her dances. In 1900 the family relocated to the French capital where Duncan continued studying Greek art at the Louvre. She performed her creative works at a variety of venues in the city—from private drawing rooms to the Théâtre du Châtelet and the former Palais du Trocadéro opposite the Eiffel Tower where the Palais du Chaillot now stands. Duncan opened several dance schools where she emphasized the importance of improvisation and emotion to her students. She suffered several personal tragedies in her life, including a freak 1913 car accident which resulted in the drowning death of her two young children in the Seine. Similarly, in September 1927 Duncan was killed in Nice when her long scarf wrapped around the wheels of her convertible.

Addresses for Duncan

- 4, rue de la Gaîté (14th)—Duncan and her family first lived above a noisy all-night printing shop at this address

- 45, avenue de Villiers (17th)—they then rented a larger studio here where Isadora gave performances for French statesman Clemenceau and sculptors Rodin and Bourdelle, among others

- 5, rue Danton (6th)—in 1909 she opened her own dance school in this building, reserving the ground floor for her living quarters

- Théâtre des Champs-Élysées at 15, avenue Montaigne (8th)— Bourdelle used Duncan's face as the model for friezes outside this theatre; her likeness also appears in Maurice Denis's murals of nine muses inside the theater's auditorium

- 103, rue la Pompe (16th)—in 1919 she turned this house into a dance studio

- 9, rue Delambre (14th)—in her mid-40s and on the verge of poverty, Duncan rented an apartment in this art deco building, purportedly dancing every day in the nearby Luxembourg Gardens

- Père Lachaise, 16, rue du Repos (20th)—Duncan's ashes are interred next to her children's in niche 6796 at this cemetery

Duke Ellington (1899-1974)

Edward Kennedy Ellington received his noble nickname as a youth due to his elegant dress and manners, a style he maintained throughout life. But it was in a pool hall, where all levels of society mixed, that pianists inspired the future band leader to take music seriously. In fact, Ellington refused an art scholarship to Pratt Institute in Brooklyn to play at clubs in his hometown of Washington D.C. Several unsuccessful attempts for his band to become part of the New York jazz scene were followed by a four-year gig at a club on West 49th Street in 1923. A few years later, weekly radio broadcasts from Harlem's Cotton Club gave Ellington's band national exposure. Touring abroad in 1933 brought them to the London and Paris. Ellington loved the City of Light especially the *joie de vivre* of Parisians. They repaid the sentiment in kind by flocking to his three concerts at the 3000-seat Salle Pleyel. The whole experience proved a positive changing point in the band's self-image. As Ellington put it: "The entire first European tour in 1933 was a tremendous uplift for all our spirits." He and Billy Strayhorn were back for an extended period in the winter of 1960-61 writing the score for the film *Paris Blues* for which Ellington received an Academy Award nomination.

Addresses for Ellington

- Salle Pleyel, 252, Faubourg Saint-Honoré (8th)—Ellington's band appeared at this Parisian concert hall in late July and early August 1933

- Bricktop's, 66, rue Jean-Baptiste Pigalle (9th)—after the second evening's concert, band members went to hear music at this former cabaret in Montmartre

- Hôtel George V, 31, avenue George V (8th)—Ellington's suite at this lavish hotel was so large and strangely arranged that he joked about having trouble finding his way out of it

- Le Tournon, 18, rue de Tournon (6th)—Ellington and band members patronized and sometimes performed at this café near the Luxembourg Gardens

- Hôtel de la Trémoille, 14, rue de la Trémoille (8th)—he and his longtime collaborator Billy Strayhorn (see his entry later in the chapter) wrote the Academy Award-nominated track for the film *Paris Blues* at this hotel during the winter of 1960-61

- L'Olympia, 28, boulevard des Capucines (9th)—in February 1963 Ellington played and recorded his *Great Paris Concert* at this music hall

Loie Fuller (1862-1928)

The innovative modern dance pioneer, known in the French capital as *La Fée Lumière* (The Fairy of Light), used to say in interviews "I was born in America, but I was made in Paris." How true that was. Young Marie Louise Fuller grew up in Chicago and at nineteen got a job touring the vaudeville circuit with Buffalo Bill Cody. Although she had no formal training as a dancer, she later began experimenting with choreography in Brooklyn using bamboo sticks, yards of material, and innovative lighting to create her routines. But it was in Paris in the fall of 1892 that her *Serpentine Dance*—and over a hundred-twenty subsequent numbers—made her a smash success. Her popular performances drew people from all walks of life: scientists like the Curies, French authors, and architect Hector Guimard. A celebrated French poet Stéphane Mallarmé referred to Fuller's act as "the theatrical form of poetry par excellence." She seemed to show up everywhere. Fuller was asked to pose for artists such as Rodin and Toulouse-Lautrec; she appeared on posters in her flowing attire; her face was even carved into the front of a building near the Arts et Métiers métro stop. Isadora Duncan, who toured Europe with Fuller's company, would go on to eclipse her mentor in popularity.

Addresses for Fuller

- Opéra Garnier, 8, rue Scribe (9ᵗʰ)—Fuller had a brief initial engagement dancing at this Paris opera house
- Folies Bergère, 32, rue Richer (9ᵗʰ)—she was a triumph from her debut at this cabaret on November 5, 1892
- L'Olympia, 28, boulevard des Capucines (9ᵗʰ)—Fuller performed at the inauguration of this famous music hall in 1893
- 39, rue Réaumur (3ʳᵈ)—a double image of her face is found on the upper floors of the façade of this building
- 29, boulevard de la Saussaye (just past the 17ᵗʰ in Neuilly)—at her home here in 1908 she founded a school of dance, Les Ballets Loïe Fuller, which emphasized "natural dancing"
- Hôtel Plaza Athénée, 25, avenue Montaigne (8ᵗʰ)—she died in a friend's room at this luxury hotel
- Père Lachaise, 16, rue du Repos (20ᵗʰ)—like Isadora Duncan, Fuller's ashes are interred at this cemetery

George Gershwin (1898-1937)

Termed "a genius" by a piano teacher when he was just a child, Gershwin was no flash in the pan. In his short life, he gained international recognition by composing such pieces such as "Rhapsody in Blue" and "An American in Paris." The Brooklyn native first learned to play by observing the moving keys on a friend's player piano and took lessons starting at age ten. Never a fan of school, he dropped out as a teenager and got a job as a song-plugger on Tin Pan Alley in Manhattan. After hitting it big at nineteen with "Swanee," famously performed by Al Jolson, Gershwin began working on Broadway. On a first trip to the French capital in April 1926, he stayed with friends Mabel and Bob Schirmer while working on "An American in Paris." He and Mabel even scrounged around garages on the avenue de la Grande Armée behind the Arc de Triomphe to buy old taxi horns to incorporate into his piece. Gershwin wanted to learn composition from composer Maurice Ravel, who reportedly replied "Why should you be a second-rate Ravel when you can be a first-rate Gershwin?" Famed music teacher Nadia Boulanger also refused him as a student fearing that classical training would ruin his jazz style.

Addresses for Gershwin

- Hôtel Majestic (now The Peninsula), 19, avenue Kléber (16th)—Gershwin and his siblings spent several months at this hotel in 1928

- Lapérouse, 51, quai des Grands Augustins (6th)—they had dinner at this restaurant which is still in business today

- 179, rue de la Pompe (16th)—in May 1928 American Gladys Byfield held a party and Gershwin concert at her home at this address for over two hundred people, including Nadia Boulanger, Man Ray, and Sylvia Beach

Quincy Jones (1933-)

If only known as the producer/arranger of Michael Jackson's *Thriller* album, Jones would be plenty famous. But the work he has done with the greatest American musicians has stretched across several decades and has been rewarded with twenty-seven Grammy awards. His career path with extremely talented performers dates back to his teen years. Jones pestered jazz great Clark Terry to give him trumpet lessons and he began an early, lifelong friendship with Ray Charles. In 1957, as Jones tells it, he went to Paris "for two weeks and stayed for five years." Actually, he came close to giving up his passport for his adopted country which he considered "a second home." Shortly after arriving in the capital, the brilliant twenty-four-year-old Jones got a job as musical director for the French company Barclay Records. Wanting to improve his skills, he became a student of Nadia Boulanger. Instead of studying classical music, though, she encouraged him to "mine the ore you already have." Jones also learned from his famed teacher that humanity shines through in your work: "Your music can only be as good, more or less, as you are as a human being," she told him. In 2014 Jones was awarded the highest rank of Chevalier des Arts et des Lettres (Knight of Arts and Letters) by the French government.

Addresses for Jones

- Conservatoire de Paris, 209, avenue Jean Jaurès (19ᵗʰ)—Jones studied musical composition and theory at the Paris Conservatory

- 36, rue Ballu (9ᵗʰ)—he auditioned for celebrated composition and counterpoint professor Nadia Boulanger at her home at this address

- The Living Room, then located at 25, rue du Colisée (8ᵗʰ)—Jones and pianist Blossom Dearie used to hang out at this former jazz club

- Théâtre des Champs-Élysées, 15, avenue Montaigne (8ᵗʰ)—at this theatre in July 2000 Jones directed the Orchestre National de France

- Hôtel George V, 31, avenue George V (8ᵗʰ)—he usually stays at this luxurious hotel when he visits Paris

Eartha Kitt (1927-2008)

From dancer to singer to "Catwoman" in the 1967 Batman TV series, Kitt was quite the versatile entertainer. Today, she is probably best remembered for her sexy renditions of songs such as "Santa Baby" and "C'est Si Bon." Talk about an all-American success story…Kitt was born out of wedlock on a cotton plantation in a small town in South Carolina and was bounced around among relatives. By age twenty, though, she became the featured dancer and vocalist in the Katherine Dunham Dance Company. The all-black cast performed their Bal Nègre throughout North America and Europe and arrived in Paris in 1949. Kitt decided to leave the troupe, though, after a nightclub owner saw her performances and offered her a job in the city. Often compared to Josephine Baker, she was a star who amused and endeared herself to French audiences especially when she began ad libbing forgotten lyrics. Wearing outfits from haute couture designers, such as Schiaparelli and Balmain, Kitt attracted the attention of many men. Actor/director Orson Welles, who caught her show a couple of times, called her "the most exciting woman in the world." In *Time Runs*, a play presented by Welles on the Right Bank, Kitt stole the show in her role as Helen of Troy.

Addresses for Kitt

- Le Carroll's, 36, rue de Ponthieu (8th)—Kitt performed at this one-time nightclub just off the Champs-Élysées

- Le Perroquet (now Chez Régine), 49, rue de Ponthieu (8th)—she had a starring role at this club that the owner opened just down the street from Le Carroll's

- Maxim's, 3, rue Royale (8th)—Dominican playboy Porfirio Rubirosa courted Kitt with champagne and caviar at this chic restaurant

- Mars Club, 6, rue Robert Estienne (8th), now Les Innocents—Kitt played some impromptu spots at this club near the Champs-Élysées.

- Hôtel Gallia, 63, rue Pierre Charron (8th)—she was staying at this former hotel in 1950 when Orson Welles asked her to audition for the role of Helen of Troy in his one-act play *Time Runs* which opened at the Théâtre des Mathurins, 36, rue des Mathurins (8th) in June 1950

- Le Calavados, 40, avenue Pierre 1er de Serbie (8th)—she and Welles frequented this club which is still in operation

Jim Morrison (1943-1971)

The "rock poet," known for songs like "Light My Fire" and "Love Me Two Times," achieved fame and fortune in his lifetime. But his mysterious death in Paris at age twenty-seven elevated Morrison to cult status. A native of Melbourne, Florida, he studied film-making at

U.C.L.A. When a college friend suggested setting some of Morrison's poems to music, they formed the rock band The Doors, whose name refers to opening the doors of perception through drug use. Morrison's own addictions quickly began to interfere with his performances. Ultimately, after a concert in Miami, he was fined and sentenced to six months in prison for profanity and indecent exposure. While the case was under appeal, Morrison decided to focus on his writing in the French capital. In March 1971 he joined his girlfriend Pam Courson who had arrived in the city earlier. Besides drinking and scoring drugs, Morrison spent time strolling by the Seine, admiring the city's architecture, and writing poetry at spots like the place des Vosges. Less than four months after he arrived, however, he was found dead in the bathtub of his rented apartment in the Marais. No foul play was suspected so no autopsy was performed. French police suspected Morrison died elsewhere from a drug overdose before being brought home.

Addresses for Morrison

- Hôtel George V, 31, avenue George V (8th)—on his first trip to Paris in June 1970 he took a room for a few days at this expensive, five-star hotel

- Hôtel Médicis, 214, rue Saint-Jacques (5th)—a month later Morrison opted for more modest quarters at this address, ironically now a swanky boutique hotel renamed Le Petit Paris

- 17-19, rue Beautrellis (4th)—Morrison and girlfriend Pamela Courson rented an apartment from a friend at this address; he was found dead in the bathtub here on July 3rd, 1971

- Le Café de Flore, 172, boulevard Saint Germain; Les Deux Magots, 6, place Saint-Germain-des-Prés, and La Palette at 43, rue de Seine (all in the 6th); La Coupole, 102, boulevard du Montparnasse (14th)—the couple frequented these popular cafés

- The Mazet, 61, rue Saint-André des Arts (6th)—Morrison was spotted at this small bar on the last day of his life

- Père Lachaise, 16, rue du Repos (20ᵗʰ)—his grave, one of the most visited sites in this cemetery, is in the sixth division; it's quite hard to find so check it out online beforehand to help you find your way

Madeleine Peyroux (1974-)

"If you like Billie Holiday, try Madeleine Peyroux," urged *The New York Times* in 2013. Yes, very true: the singer-songwriter, who found international acclaim with her *Careless Love* album, recalls the elegant vocal style of Lady Day. As a child in Athens, Georgia, young Maddie used to listen to everything from Hank Williams to Ravel in her father's record collection. She soon picked up the ukulele and began playing the guitar by age twelve. After her parents' divorce in 1987, she moved with her mother and brother to Saint-Germain-en-Laye, west of Paris. They then relocated downtown near place de la République (11ᵗʰ). While the teenager was originally against leaving her home country, Peyroux later decided it was "like going to heaven, a second life." That second life entailed skipping school to busk on city streets. Peyroux asked to join a jazz band called The Riverboat Shufflers where she was first relegated to passing the hat for coins but soon began performing. At sixteen she was touring Europe with The Lost Wandering Blues and Jazz Band and in her early twenties was discovered by an Atlantic Records talent scout in Manhattan. Peyroux put songs from her early busking years on her debut CD, *Dreamland,* which drew rave reviews from *Time* magazine.

Addresses for Peyroux

- The Mazet, 61, rue Saint-André des Arts (6ᵗʰ)—at age fifteen Peyroux was singing outside of this small bar in the Latin Quarter

- Le Bilboquet, once at 13, rue Saint-Benoît (6ᵗʰ)—her group, The Riverboat Shufflers, had their first indoor gig at this jazz club

- rue de l'Abbaye (6ᵗʰ)—tourists remember hearing the young woman sing in a small park on this street off the rue Bonaparte

- L'Olympia, 28, boulevard des Capucines (9ᵗʰ)—a big star in May

2013, Peyroux performed at this famed music hall

Cole Porter (1891-1964)

"I Love Paris in the winter when it drizzles, I love Paris in the summer when it sizzles." Porter, like his song, was a true fan of the city and appreciated its World War I-era inhabitants who were "so attractive, so amusing, so wonderfully brave, and so simple." The Peru, Indiana native's fondness for the capital began when his grandfather rewarded him with a trip to Europe for being named valedictorian at boarding school. An English major at Yale, he gave Harvard Law a try before transferring to the school's music department. After a musical flopped on Broadway, a humiliated Porter moved to Paris in 1917, ostensibly to join the French Foreign Legion. Instead, the wealthy young man enjoyed living the high life and reconnecting with Yale buddies like Archie MacLeish. At the time of his marriage to socialite Linda Thomas, gossip columnist Walter Winchell described the couple as: "Boy with $1 million weds girl with $2 million." Who else could afford the half-timbered home they bought in central Paris? It featured, among other things, platinum wallpaper, zebra-skin rugs, and apple trees in the yard. The *Colporteurs* ("street vendors"), as they were ironically called because of the sound-alike French word, maintained that Left Bank residence for twenty years. The couple's marriage was by all accounts happy despite Cole's homosexuality. Their extravagant parties, which sometimes lasted for days, included entertainers such as "Bricktop" Ada Smith who taught guests the Charleston and other popular dances of the time.

Addresses for Porter

- Van Cleef & Arpels, 22, place Vendôme (1ˢᵗ)—Porter often played the piano at this jewelry store

- Hôtel Ritz, 15, place Vendôme (1ˢᵗ)—he met divorcée Linda Lee Thomas, eight years his senior, at a wedding at this luxury hotel in January 1918

- La Mairie du XVIIIe Arrondissement, 1, place Jules Joffrin

(18ᵗʰ)—Porter and Thomas got married at the town hall of the 18ᵗʰ arrondissement nearly two years later

- 3, rue de la Baume (8ᵗʰ)—the couple first lived in Linda's small house off the boulevard Haussmann, while maintaining a suite at the Ritz

- 13, rue Monsieur (7ᵗʰ)—they then bought a lavish ten-bedroom, six-bathroom house behind an unassuming façade at this location near Les Invalides

- Bricktop's, once located at 66, rue Jean-Baptiste Pigalle (9ᵗʰ)— Porter frequented this famous cabaret in Montmartre and even composed the song "Miss Otis Regrets" for Bricktop, Ada Smith herself (see her entry later in this chapter)

- Schola Cantorum, 269, rue Saint-Jacques (5ᵗʰ)—thinking he wanted to write classical music, Porter enrolled at this private music school…until he decided that the instruction interfered with his sense of rhythm

Nina Simone (1933-2003)

"The High Priestess of Soul" began her life as Eunice Waymon in the tiny town of Tryon, North Carolina. Her stage name, adopted to avoid embarrassing her mother by performing "the devil's music" in a bar, combined a teenaged nickname with that of French actress Simone Signoret. The future jazz legend discovered the piano early on and, with community funding, studied at Juilliard. Denied entrance to Philadelphia's Curtis Institute, she took a job in Atlantic City where the owner forced her to sing while playing the piano. This was the push her career needed and led to an album with Bethlehem Records in 1957 and stardom in Manhattan two years later. Depressed and bitter about racism, she wrote the songs "To Be Young, Gifted and Black" to support the civil rights movement and "Mississipppi Goddam" after the killings of African-Americans in the South. When the public shunned Simone for her political activism, she relocated to several different countries before, she says, "I went to Paris thinking I could resume my career." Financially drained and suffering from mental illness, she began performing at a nearly empty Latin Quarter café: "I was desperate and no one believed that I was there…no one came to see me…I had fallen from grace." Soon, though, word got around and her erratic but often magical performances drew sold-out crowds every night for a year.

Addresses for Simone

- Novotel, 1, avenue de la République— in the early 1980s Simone was staying at this hotel just outside the 20th arrondissement in Bagnolet when Jacques Boni approached her about playing at his small club, Aux Trois Mailletz, 56, rue Galande (5th) where she performed for a year

- Villa du Parc Montsouris, 8-12, rue Émile-Deutsch-de-La-Meurthe (14th)—Boni leased a 3-bedroom apartment for Simone in this cul-de-sac across from the park of the same name

- InterContinental Paris Le Grand Hôtel, 2, rue Scribe (9th)— increasingly belligerent, she nearly slugged a total stranger in the lobby of this hotel

- L'Olympia, 28, boulevard des Capucines (9th)—this famous music hall hosted sold-out performances several times during Simone's career

Ada "Bricktop" Smith (1894-1984)

No longer a name familiar to most Americans, the charming, cigar-smoking, feather boa-wearing nightclub owner was once the toast of Montmartre. Nicknamed Bricktop because of the flaming red hair and freckles from her Irish side, Smith was born into poverty in Alderson, West Virginia. She quit school in Chicago at sixteen to tour as a dancer with an African-American vaudeville company. After becoming a huge success at the popular Connie's Inn in Harlem, she was offered a job at Le Grand Duc (The Great Duke) in Paris in 1924. Despite its grandiose name, the twelve-table establishment in Montmartre proved a crushing disappointment for Smith. She was consoled by the cabaret's dishwasher, none other than aspiring poet Langston Hughes (see his entry in Chapter 5). Two years later the enterprising woman opened her own nightclub, Chez Bricktop, which became a smash hit, attracting a long list of international expatriates. Sidney Bechet, Duke Ellington, and Django Reinhardt played at times in "Brickie's" band and Cole Porter composed her theme song, "Miss Otis Regrets." Smith visited with nearly everyone at her club—Josephine Baker, Kay Boyle, Man Ray, Scott Fitzgerald, and Elsa Maxwell, to name but a few. She taught popular American dances like the Charleston and the Black Bottom to anyone interested, including the Duke and Duchess of Windsor.

Addresses for Smith

- Le Grand Duc, once at 52, rue Jean-Baptiste Pigalle (9th)—in 1924 Bricktop left large clubs in New York for this small venue formerly at the intersection of the rue Pierre Fontaine

- 66, rue Jean-Baptiste Pigalle (9th)—she soon opened her own club which changed locations a few times before settling at this address, now a modern building

- 36, rue Jean-Baptiste Pigalle (9th)—Smith first lived at this address in Montmartre; in 1929 she moved to 47, avenue Trudaine (9th) and six years later took an apartment at 35, rue Victor Massé (9th)

- 13, rue Monsieur (7th)—Cole Porter invited her to teach the latest dances to guests at parties in his extravagant home on the Left Bank

Billy Strayhorn (1915-1967)

Duke Ellington once referred to his close friend and longtime collaborator as "my right arm, my left arm, all the eyes in the back of my head." A native of Dayton, Ohio, Strayhorn spent years at his grandparents' home in North Carolina where he listened to his grandmother's records and the hymns she played on the piano. By high school he was composing songs such as "Lush Life" whose lyrics reveal an early attraction to the City of Light. Because opportunities in his first love, classical music, were slim at the time for African-Americans, Strayhorn turned to jazz. After meeting Duke Ellington in December 1938, he wrote his most famous tune "Take the A Train" based on instructions to the bandleader's New York home. Strayhorn's decades-long involvement with Ellington's band included work as a composer, arranger, and sometime pianist. The duo even teamed up to produce soundtracks for films such as *Paris Blues* which they composed at a hotel in the city. Ellington remembered that "Strayhorn loved Paris …it was one of his favorite places." Strays or Swee' Pea, as he was called because of his diminutive size and mild manner, was quite the dapper guy who enjoyed shopping in the stylish shops of the capital.

Addresses for Strayhorn

- L'Olympia, 28, boulevard des Capucines (9th)— Strayhorn and Ellington played with the band at this famous music hall on several different occasions

- Hôtel de la Trémoille, 14, rue de la Trémoille (8th)—during the winter of 1960-61 the duo stayed at this hotel while writing the score for the film *Paris Blues*

- Mars Club, now Les Innocents, 6, rue Robert Estienne (8th)— Strayhorn often went to hear the house pianist and former lover Aaron Bridgers, play at this Right Bank club; other favorites included Bricktop's formerly at 66, rue Jean-Baptiste Pigalle (9th) in Montmartre and the Club Saint-Germain, once at 13, rue Saint-Benoît (6th)

- Hôtel Claridge, 74, avenue des Champs-Élysées (8th)—he enjoyed shopping at luxury boutiques at this hotel or at the gourmet food shop Fauchon, 24-26, place de la Madeleine (8th)—both still in operation

- Café de la Paix, 5, place de l'Opéra (9th)—Strayhorn and Orson Welles worked on songs for the play *Time Runs* at this chic restaurant across from the Opéra Garnier

Chapter 11

Other Important Americans

SOME FAMOUS AMERICANS WHO chose Paris as their one-time home don't fit neatly into any of the previous categories. But who could imagine leaving out former First Lady Jacqueline Kennedy or television's legendary "French Chef" Julia Child? So, into a special chapter they go, along with a somewhat motley mixture of others. For starters, you can't get more varied than *Joan of Arc* and *Breathless* actress Jean Seberg (who is actually buried in Montparnasse Cemetery), educator and women's rights champion Emma Willard, and supreme party-giver Elsa Maxwell, "the Hostess with the Mostest." Three outstanding physicians who chose to continue their studies in the French capital take their place this section: Oliver Wendell Holmes, Sr., who was also a poet; Elizabeth Blackwell, the first American female doctor; and Mary Putnam Jacobi, the first woman admitted to the Parisian medical school, l'École de Médecine. Two wealthy American patrons of arts also made the list: art collector Peggy Guggenheim and Harry Crosby, both sometime poets as well. In all, you will discover ten hard-to-pin-down but quite interesting individuals in the following pages.

Elizabeth Blackwell (1821-1910)

Talk about someone who wouldn't take no for an answer! Rejections from twenty-nine American medical schools did not deter the

British-born woman from her dream of becoming the first female doctor in the United States. Blackwell was finally accepted into Geneva Medical College in upstate New York and graduated at the top of her class in 1849. She then decided to continue her education abroad. Physicians back home warned her of the "fearful immorality" she would face as a single woman in Paris…not to mention the plague and cholera raging there at the time. Nevertheless, Dr. Blackwell took the plunge and enjoyed "a constant effervescence of life" in the French capital. Once again, however, she was rebuffed in her efforts to enter medical school—unless she agreed to disguise herself as a man. Instead, she opted for lectures at the *Collège de France* and the *Jardin des Plantes* (5ᵗʰ) and ultimately enrolled in midwifery courses at *La Maternité de Port Royal*. At the maternity hospital she taught others about current views on the prevention of childbed fever. A serious infection she contracted from an infant patient led to the removal of her left eye, ending her hopes of practicing surgery. For the next six months, she recovered at her sister Anna's apartment near the Luxembourg Gardens. In 1851 Blackwell returned to New York City where she practiced medicine and opened a medical college for women.

Addresses for Blackwell

- 11, rue de Seine (6ᵗʰ)—after a brief stay in a hotel, Blackwell found an affordable room at this Left Bank address

- La Maternité de Paris Port-Royal, 53, avenue de l'Observatoire (14ᵗʰ)—she enrolled in midwife classes and lived in a dismal dormitory here; the name of the maternity hospital can be seen carved above the doorway at the southwest corner of boulevard de Port-Royal at rue du Faubourg Saint-Jacques

- rue de Fleurus (6ᵗʰ) [no number]—after the accident which caused the loss of an eye, Blackwell moved in with her sister Anna in an apartment overlooking the Luxembourg Gardens

Julia Child (1912-2004)

Plain and simple: some people need no introduction. Such is the case of *The French Chef* author and PBS television personality largely responsible for introducing French cuisine to Americans. Born Julia McWilliams in Pasadena, California, she attended Smith College in Massachusetts with the intention of becoming a novelist. At 6'2" she was too tall to join the military during World War II and served her country working for the Office of Strategic Services in Washington, D. C. Sent to Sri Lanka for her job, she became friends with and later married Paul Child who shared her love of music and, very importantly, food. In November 1948 the State Department transferred her husband to Paris. En route from Le Havre, the young woman had an epiphany while eating her first French meal in the city of Rouen. This experience would ultimately shape the direction of her life. For her thirty-seventh birthday in August of the next year, her husband bought her a copy of the culinary bible *Larousse Gastronomique*. Two months later she enrolled at the world-renowned Cordon Bleu cooking school. With two French friends Child began adapting French recipes into a cookbook, the classic *Mastering the Art of French Cooking*. The rest, shall we say, is culinary history. In 2000 France awarded Julia Child its highest honor, the Légion d'honneur.

Addresses for Child

- Hôtel Pont Royal, 5-7, rue Montalembert (7th)—the couple first had a room at this hotel which is still in operation

- 81, rue de l'Université (7th)—in early December 1948 the Childs moved to an apartment on the second and third floors at this address on the "Roo de Loo," as they called it, near the Palais Bourbon, the seat of the French National Assembly

- 129, rue du Faubourg Saint-Honoré (8th)—in the fall of the next year Child began taking cooking classes at the Cordon Bleu (now located at 13-15, quai André Citroën in the 15th), which was run by the disagreeable Madame Élisabeth Brassart

- 18-20, rue Coquillière (1ˢᵗ)—she was a regular shopper at E. Dehillerin, a kitchen store which has been at this address since 1890

- Les Deux Magots and the Brasserie Lipp, opposite each other on the boulevard Saint-Germain (6ᵗʰ), and Le Grand Véfour at 17, rue de Beaujolais (1ˢᵗ)—the couple enjoyed eating out at cafés and restaurants such as these which are still open for business; the lovely and very expensive Grand Véfour is just right for Snobs

Harry Crosby (1898-1929)

No relation to crooner Bing of "White Christmas" fame, this Crosby was a Boston Brahmin and heir to a vast banking fortune. For most of his short life, which, like that of his friend Hart Crane, ended in suicide, Crosby symbolized what Gertrude Stein termed "the Lost Generation." During World War I, he escaped the strictures of his socially prominent parents by serving as an ambulance driver in France . This experience gave him a morbid fascination with death. Crosby then married Polly Peabody, a divorced mother of two, and moved his family to Paris for seven years. The couple led "a mad and extravagant life" full of orgies, gambling, drugs, caviar, oysters, and gallons of champagne. Their charm and good looks attracted the attention of other expatriates including authors Ernest Hemingway and Archie MacLeish. Frustrated at trying to get their own literary works published, the Crosbys opened Black Sun Press where they also printed pieces by Ezra Pound, D. H. Lawrence, and James Joyce, among others. In 1928 the couple leased an old building named Le Moulin du Soleil (The Sun Mill) in Ermenonville about an hour's drive northeast of the French capital where they continued their decadent ways with friends such as Crane, Kay Boyle, and Salvador Dalí.

Addresses for Crosby

- 12, quai d'Orléans (4ᵗʰ)—Crosby and his family first took an apartment at this address on the Île Saint-Louis

- Morgan, Harjes et Cie, 14, place Vendôme (1ˢᵗ)—his wife Polly, aka Caresse, sporting a red bathing suit, would often row him down the Seine to his job at this investment bank

- 71, rue du Faubourg Saint-Honoré (8th)—the couple leased an apartment from a friend at this location; they then relocated to 29, rue Boulard (14th) after Crosby quit his job to become a full-time poet and publisher

- 19, rue de Lille (7th)—in November 1925 they ultimately settled into a stylish apartment with a sunken marble tub at this address

- 2, rue Cardinale (6th)—their publishing house, Black Sun Press, was located near their apartment

Peggy Guggenheim (1898-1979)

This fabulously wealthy heiress had a passion for collecting things—most notably lovers and works of art. Young Marguerite grew up in the privileged yet oppressive atmosphere of Manhattan's Upper East Side. As a child, during her family's annual summer trips to Europe, she developed a love for Paris. The young woman got to know members of New York's bohemian elite while working at an avant-garde bookstore in Greenwich Village. After her businessman father Benjamin died on the Titanic, Peggy inherited a fortune and in 1920 decided to live the high life in the French capital. Two years later Guggenheim married Laurence Vail who introduced her to various members of the art world, including photographer Man Ray and artist Salvador Dalí. Guggenheim regularly attended Natalie Barney's literary salon and became the patron of *Nightwood* author Djuna Barnes. One paramour, Irish-born author Samuel Beckett, encouraged Guggenheim to start buying modern art. So, in 1937 aided by French artist Marcel Duchamp, she purchased her first painting. As the Nazis approached the city during World War II, Guggenheim was on a mission to "buy one picture a day." This decision led to an extensive collection which became the source of an art museum now located in Venice.

Addresses for Guggenheim

- Hôtel de Crillon, 10, place de la Concorde and later the Hôtel

Plaza-Athénée, 25, avenue Montaigne (both in the 8th)—when she first moved to Paris, Guggenheim took rooms at these luxury hotels

- La Mairie, 71, avenue Henri-Martin (16th)—in 1922 she married artist/writer Laurence Vail in the town hall of the 16th arrondissement

- Hôtel Lutetia, 45, boulevard Raspail (6th)—the couple took rooms at this lavish Left Bank hotel

- 55, avenue Reille (14th)—Guggenheim and her British lover John Holms leased this house not far from the Parc Montsouris

- Le Bœuf sur le Toit, celebrated cabaret once located at 26, rue de Penthièvre (8th), now at 34, rue du Colisée; Bricktop's, formerly at rue Jean-Baptiste Pigalle in Montmartre (9th); Restaurant Le Fouquet's, 99, avenue des Champs-Élysées (8th)—three of Guggenheim's favorite hangouts

- 14, rue Hallé (14th)—before the outbreak of World War II, she stayed at the apartment of her friend Mary Reynolds at this address

- 12, place du Vendôme (1st)—in April 1940 Guggenheim rented a huge apartment which served as her residence and home to her ever-growing art collection

Oliver Wendell Holmes, Sr. (1809-1894)

A successful poet as well as a medical doctor, Holmes, Sr. was a true Renaissance man. In his case, however, cultivating both his literary and scientific sides was more of a problem than an asset. Even though Holmes wrote an important essay about the contagiousness of childbed fever, he was not always taken seriously as a physician. As a biographer succinctly put it: "a reputation for wit and poetry has never been known to increase a doctor's practice." Born in Cambridge, Massachusetts, Holmes graduated in classical languages and literature from Harvard in 1829. The following year he gained national recognition for his poem "Old Ironsides," which helped save the well-known frigate from being destroyed. Holmes then enrolled in a private medical school in Boston. In 1833 he got the idea of continuing his studies in the City of Light, the world center for medical training and research. Letters home during his stay reveal his love for the "paradise of Parisian life." True to form, Holmes enjoyed immersing himself in French medical advances as well as in his study of the language and culture. He wrote his father: "I love to talk French, to eat French, and to drink French every now and then." Holmes returned home in October 1885 with a professional library, some instruments, and "a box with two skeletons and some skulls."

Addresses for Holmes

- 55, rue Monsieur-le Prince (6th)—for his two-and-half years in Paris Holmes had an apartment near the Luxembourg Gardens which looked out on the rue de Vaugirard

- Hôpital Universitaire Pitié-Salpêtrière, 47-83, boulevard de l'Hôpital (13th)—a dedicated student, he spent many hours studying at this hospital

- Le Procope, 13, rue de l'Ancienne Comédie (6th)—he and other medical students from Boston gathered almost every day at this café, the oldest in Paris

- Les Trois Frères Provençaux, 8, rue de Montpensier (1st)—they often had dinner at this former restaurant in the Palais-Royal, famous for its décor and its food

- Hôtel d'Orient (now the Hôtel Daunou), 6, rue Daunou (2nd)—Holmes and his daughter Amelia stayed at this hotel on a trip to the city in 1886

Mary Corinna Putnam Jacobi (1842-1906)

Perseverance, as the saying goes, pays off. But for women wanting to become physicians in the nineteenth century, the need for stick-to-itiveness was very great indeed. Like her friend Elizabeth Blackwell, Minnie Putnam was born in England yet blazed the trail for American women in medicine. As a pharmacist in Yonkers, New York, she was supported in her quest to become a physician by her father—even though he believed this "repulsive pursuit" would undermine her femininity. Putnam first attended Philadelphia's Female Medical College but was frustrated by the rambling lectures of the professors and the lack of preparation by other students. After exploring clinical medicine at New England Hospital for Women and Children in Boston, Putnam looked to Europe for her training. Arriving in Paris in September 1866, she was "as one intoxicated" by the beauty of the city's architecture, statues, and fountains. But then her work began in earnest. Putnam rejected the midwifery school path adopted by Blackwell. She somehow finagled permission to attend clinics and lectures at two Parisian hospitals. Being an outsider in France in this case worked to her advantage. She was first accepted at the École Pratique, a research institution. Putnam then went on to become the first woman to attend the prestigious med school, l'École de Médecine, graduating with honors in 1871. In the fall of that year she returned to New York where she began practicing medicine and taught at Elizabeth Blackwell's Woman's Medical College.

Addresses for Putnam Jacobi

- 39, rue Monsieur le Prince (6th)—Elizabeth Blackwell, visiting Paris at the time, helped Putnam find a small room with Mademoiselle Clérambault on the Left Bank near the Jardin du Luxembourg

- Hôpital Lariboissière, 2, rue Ambroise (10th) and Hôpital Universitaire Pitié-Salpêtrière, 47-83, boulevard de l'Hôpital (13th)—refusing to settle for La Maternité de Port-Royal as Blackwell had done, Putnam got permission to attend lectures and clinics at these two hospitals

- L'École Pratique de la Faculté de Médecine, 15, rue de l'École de Médecine (6th)—she was accepted to this research institution before she was allowed to take courses at the medical school

- 91, rue des Feuillantines (5th)—in the fall of 1870 she moved in with her friends, the Réclus family, near the Sorbonne

Elsa Maxwell (1883-1963)

The so-called "Hostess with the Mostest" might be described in today's terms as "famous for being famous." Maxwell, a self-made party-giver *extraordinaire*, charmed her way into gigs as a gossip columnist, a regular on *Tonight Starring Jack Paar*, and her own *Party Line* radio program in Hollywood. The only child of middle-class parents in Keokuk, Iowa, Elsie left school at fourteen to work as a pianist in the theatre and vaudeville. During World War I in New York, she began throwing lavish themed parties which continued after she arrived in the French capital, "the most perfect city in the world." Maxwell felt that "Anyone who has lived, loved, and laughed in Paris must have a happier heart today." Her inventive social events included "Come as Your Opposite" (…where people dressed up as the other gender), "Come as You Were" (…when the vehicle arrived to take you to the bash), and a "Hate Party" (…where guests came as someone they most despised). The list of invitees encompassed a wide range of people from politicians to the chief of police (quite a clever move on her part), to the Duke and Duchess of Windsor, and celebrities like Marlene Dietrich. Her intimate friends included Cole Porter, Noel Coward, and Ada "Bricktop" Smith who collaborated with her on certain get-togethers.

Addresses for Maxwell

- 1, rue Gît-le-Cœur (6ᵗʰ)—Maxwell continued her partying ways in Paris when she lived "in a very old house" on the quai des Saints-Augustins

- Hôtel Ritz, 15, place Vendôme (1ˢᵗ)—in 1919 she gave a big shindig at this luxury hotel with entertainment provided by Ada "Bricktop" Smith

- Casino de Paris, 16, rue de Clichy (9ᵗʰ)—a near-riot broke out when party-goers at her 1927 scavenger hunt attempted to retrieve a slipper from the foot of a singer at this music hall

- L'Escargot d'Or, 38, rue Montorgueil (1ˢᵗ)—Maxwell enjoyed snails at this restaurant and oysters with Vouvray wine at Prunier

16, avenue Victor-Hugo (16th), both still in operation

- Acacia, 7, rue des Acacias (17th) and Le Jardin de Ma Sœur at 17, rue de Caumartin (9th)—she opened her own two Parisian cabarets formerly at these locations

Jacqueline Bouvier Kennedy Onassis (1929-1994)

One person who couldn't possibly be omitted from this list is this former First Lady, supporter of the arts, fashion icon, and well-respected book editor. She was born in Southampton, New York to a wealthy Wall Street broker father. Her paternal grandfather had written a book entitled *Our Forebears* which incorrectly maintained the family's noble origins in France but perhaps did inspire a long-lasting fascination with French culture in his granddaughter. During her junior year at Vassar in 1949, Miss Bouvier first traveled with her study abroad group to Grenoble for intensive French classes. Then, while studying in Paris, the students took up residence with French families. Looking back on the experience she said: "I loved it more than any year of my life." For an admirer of the arts, of course, the city is paradise. And the young woman took full advantage of excursions to the Louvre, the opera, the theater, and the ballet—just for starters. In the summer of 1951 after graduating from college, Bouvier took her younger sister Lee on a European tour which included a stay in the French capital. From sketches and notes made during their trip, the siblings prepared a book for their family they called *One Special Summer*.

Addresses for Onassis

- 76, avenue Mozart (16th)—during her junior year abroad, Bouvier lived with the de Renty family at this address near the Bois de Boulogne

- 4, rue de Chevreuse (6th)—she took classes at the Sorbonne and at Reid Hall formerly at this address off the boulevard du Montparnasse

- Brasserie Balzar at 49, rue des Écoles (5th)—with friends she sometimes frequented this bistro still open for business near the university

- Hôtel Ritz, 15, place Vendôme (1st)—the young Miss Bouvier went to the Ritz Bar when she wanted to feel "swanky"

- Hôtel Continental, (the present-day Westin Paris), 3, rue de Castiglione (1st)—on their European tour the Bouvier sisters stayed at this hotel off the rue de Rivoli

- 88, avenue Foch (16th)—after her marriage to shipping magnate Aristotle Onassis, she shared his fifteen-room apartment which had views of the Eiffel Tower and the Arc de Triomphe

- Hôtel Plaza-Athénée, 25, avenue Montaigne (8th)—following Onassis's death in 1975, his daughter Athina sold the avenue Foch apartment and his widow sometimes stayed at this elegant hotel on the Right Bank

- Hôtel de Crillon, 10, place de la Concorde (8th)—to provide anonymity on a business trip she once registered as "Mrs. Lancaster" at this historic hotel

Jean Seberg (1938-1979)

What happens when a vulnerable teenager from Marshalltown, Iowa has her whole world turned upside-down? For Seberg, it didn't go well. Radical changes began after she was selected from about 18,000 applicants to play the lead role in the Hollywood movie *Saint Joan*. Fame, in her case, ultimately led to a tumultuous and troubled life. On a publicity tour of Paris the eighteen year old was enthralled: "What a place and amazing people!" While working on a second Preminger film, *Bonjour Tristesse*, she met and married French lawyer turned film director François Moreuil. Living in France seemed to offer the international film star a way to enjoy the privacy she craved. On a trip to Los Angeles in December 1959, she was introduced to the French consul, Romain Gary, a celebrated novelist. Nine months later she left Moreuil for Gary who eventually became her second husband. Seberg received many accolades over her career including from renowned director François Truffaut who called her "the best actress in Europe" for her performance in *Breathless*. Publically slandered by FBI for her connection to the Black Panthers, she had several episodes of depression and suicide attempts. At age forty, Seberg was found dead in her car outside her home in the 16th arrondissement from a combination drugs and alcohol.

Addresses for Seberg

- 108, rue du Bac (7th)—from a place on the Île-Saint-Louis Seberg and writer Romain Gary moved to an opulent third-floor, twelve-room apartment at this location

- 125, rue de Longchamp (16th)—following her divorce from Gary in 1970, she lived at this address and was found dead in her car nearby from an overdose of drugs and alcohol

- Cimetière du Montparnasse, 3 boulevard Edgar Quinet (14th)— Seberg is buried in division 13 of this cemetery

Emma Hart Willard (1787-1870)

Like many women of her time, Willard possessed a "vigorous mind." But how fortunate to have a father who believed in schooling girls and a husband who encouraged her ideas for educational reform! As a teenager she attended Berlin Academy in Connecticut and became a teacher there a few years later. While working as a principal at a women's academy in Middlebury, Vermont, she married a local physician John Willard. To help with finances, Mrs. Willard opened a boarding school for women in her home which included courses in political studies, math, science, and philosophy. Her 1819 pamphlet *A Plan for Female Education* led to the creation of the first school of higher education for women in Troy, New York. The Troy Female Seminary, later renamed in her honor, was quite successful and resulted in Willard touring Europe to discuss women's education. In 1830 she and her son John arrived in Paris for a six-month stay. Although Willard found the mid-nineteenth century city a mixture of "the grand with the mean—the highly elegant with the dirty and disagreeable," she was more than delighted by gardens at the Palais Royal, the Tuileries, and the Jardin des Plantes. Willard also began a lifelong friendship with French authors Louise Swanton Belloc and Adélaïde de Montgolfier who considered her "a star and a guide."

Addresses for Willard

- L'Hôtel de l'Europe, 97, rue de Richelieu (2nd)—Willard and her son John took lodging in this former hotel near the Palais-Royal, now the location of the Passage des Princes

- L'École Impériale de Dessin et Mathématiques, 5, rue de l'École de Médecine (6th)—for a time they lived at this school where the husband of Willard's friend Louise Swanton Belloc was a professor

- 183, rue de Bourbon, now the rue de Lille (7th)—along with James Fenimore Cooper, she often dined with Lafayette at his home which was razed in the early twentieth century

Chapter 12

Americans and Café Life

CAFÉS AND RESTAURANTS, WE are happy to report, have long been and continue to be just about everywhere you look in Paris. These establishments also remain at the center of the social, intellectual, and artistic life of the city—even if the trend has diminished somewhat in recent years. This chapter concentrates on two areas of the Left Bank which were favored by famous Americans in the past: Montparnasse and Saint-Germain-des-Prés. As is normally the case, the "in" places to see and be seen evolve over the years. In the early twentieth century the cultural elite began switching their allegiance from places up on the hill in Montmartre to the southern section of Montparnasse, no doubt because of the cheaper prices then found there. Especially prized were the large restaurants and cafés straddling the 6th and 14th arrondissements along boulevard du Montparnasse, places like the Dôme, the Coupole, the Rotonde, and the Select. These locations were very popular with our compatriots—maybe a little too much in the case of heavy drinkers such as Ernest Hemingway, Scott Fitzgerald, Sinclair Lewis, and Henry Miller. Loyalties shifted once again in the period following World War II when the area of Saint Germain-des-Prés near the Seine became the place to be. The Café de Flore, Les Deux Magots, and the Tournon developed into hangouts for Americans from the intellectual, artistic, and literary communities the likes of Janet Flanner, Hart Crane, Jimmy Baldwin, and Dick Wright.

164

The following alphabetical list contains the past's most popular Left Bank hangouts, mostly still in operation under the same name today. In the interest of "investigating Parisian culture," no trip to the city would be complete without lingering over a cup of espresso or a glass of wine at an outdoor terrace. So, try your best to do some "research" at one or more of these watering holes. Just be sure to verify the hours of operation before you go. And if you're still thirsty, drop in at Le Falstaff, tucked away at 42, rue du Montparnasse, just off the wide boulevard of the same name. This small beer pub, which is open nearly all night, was once the scene of an infamous 1929 boxing match. It seems that an inattentive or, most likely, drunken Scott Fitzgerald failed to sound the final bell before Ernest Hemingway was thoroughly pummeled by fellow journalist Morley Callaghan. Now that deserves a drink. Cheers!

In Montparnasse:
La Closerie des Lilas, 171, boulevard du Montparnasse (RER Port-Royal, 6th)

What better place to start your exploration than this pretty spot named for its lilac trees? When it first opened in 1847, it was a stopover for thirsty travelers on the carriage route to Fontainebleau, southeast of the capital. Popularity grew by leaps and bounds when patrons began dropping in on a trip to the former garden ballroom, the Bal Bullier, across the street. Over the years the brasserie has hosted its fair share of French and international authors, artists, and intellectuals like Monet, Picasso, and even Russian revolutionary Vladimir Lenin. Prominent Americans including Hart Crane, John Dos Passos, Scott Fitzgerald, Man Ray, A. J. Liebling, and Dorothy Parker patronized it as well. Just a five-minute walk from his apartment on Notre-Dame-des-Champs, American poet Ezra Pound often came by. So did his neighbor Ernest Hemingway who spent so much time writing and socializing at this café that even today a brass plaque bearing his name can be found on its polished wooden bar. La Closerie des Lilas was also the place Hemingway first received a copy of *The Great Gatsby* from Scott Fitzgerald. A decade later author Henry Miller continued the tradition and did his work at these tables as well. Divided into two parts—an upscale restaurant and a less-expensive brasserie with nightly live jazz—the café is open daily from 12:00 to 2:30 and 7:00 to 11:30 p.m.

La Coupole, 102, boulevard du Montparnasse (métro Vavin, 14th)

The "new kid on the block" was once the site of an old wood and charcoal yard. In 1927 it was transformed into a chic eatery by the previous managers of the popular eatery the Dôme a few doors down. As a way of attracting clients, they cleverly chose the name La Coupole, synonymous with their former place of business. In another shrewd move, for the grand opening of the huge 600-seat space the managers footed the bill for free appetizers and popped 1500 bottles of champagne. American artist/photographer Man Ray was among the thousands of invitees, the last of whom had to be chased away by the police at five o'clock in the morning. Among the thirty-two Art Deco interior pillars—decorated by French artists of the day—is a tribute to performer Josephine Baker surrounded by ostrich feathers in the back right of the dining room. Baker used to arrive accompanied by one of her various lovers and often her pet cheetah Chiquita until the owners told her the animal frightened the clientele. Hemingway, searching for material for his books, patronized this café as did fellow Americans Kay Boyle, Lawrence Ferlinghetti, Katherine Anne Porter, and, years later, The Doors rocker Jim Morrison. Novelist Henry Miller was a regular who stopped by for breakfast in the 1930s. Refurbished to its former glory in 1988, the restaurant is now open for business from 8:00 a.m. till 11:00 p.m.

Dingo Bar, now Auberge de Venise, 10, rue Delambre (métro Vavin, 14th)

No list of Parisian watering holes would be complete without this location, so popular with Americans of the past. The once disreputable dive has not only changed names but has been miraculously transformed into an upstanding Italian restaurant. Still, there remains a fittingly preserved remnant: the old wooden bar familiar to the heavy-drinking members of the "Lost Generation." The Dingo began attracting crowds nearly immediately after its opening in 1923 since it was one of the few places open for business all night long. And, of course, many American expats found their way here around the corner from the larger cafés on the boulevard du Montparnasse. In April 1925 it was the scene of the historic first meeting between literary lions Scott Fitzgerald and Ernest Hemingway. A few years later, dance pioneer Isadora Duncan, who had moved into an apartment building across the street at number 9, began dropping by. A long list of American writers from John Dos Passos, Ezra Pound, Sinclair Lewis, Sherwood Anderson, and Thornton Wilder to Henry Miller and Dorothy Parker discovered the Dingo over the years as well. Author Djuna Barnes was friends with its famed bartender, Jimmie Charters, a former British boxer who was at least partly responsible for the bar's huge success. The Auberge de Venise, no longer a drop-in-for-a-drink kind of place, serves meals from 11:00 a.m. to 3:00 p.m. and 7:00 p.m. to 11:30 p.m., till 1:00 a.m. on the weekend.

Le Dôme, 108, boulevard du Montparnasse (métro Vavin, 14ᵗʰ)

A hangout for starving artists and authors no more—not at all! Since its opening way back in 1898, this landmark café has slowly transformed to the Michelin-starred restaurant it is today. In the early 1900s, though, anyone with a few francs could have the daily special or a drink with friends while enjoying a game of pool, chess, or cards. In 1928 the owner increased its clientele by adding "American Bar" to the outdoor awning to attract, among others, those fleeing Prohibition in the States. And what an amazing group passed through its doors. Hemingway preferred the hard-working regulars here to the pretentious crowd at La Rotonde across the street. Photographer Man Ray and his model/girlfriend Kiki de Montparnasse were at this café so often that they had a regularly reserved table. Alexander Calder used to drop by in the afternoon to discuss art with international pals such as Joan Miró and Piet Mondrian. Several decades later, the Dôme was a favorite of columnist Art Buchwald. The long and impressive list of American customers through the years includes Lawrence Ferlinghetti, Sinclair Lewis, Henry Miller, Katherine Anne Porter, Ezra Pound, Glenway Wescott, and William Carlos Williams, to name but a few. So, give the place a look, but keep in mind that a delicious plate of sole will cost you about fifty euros! For Snobs only these days. Le Dôme is open daily from every day from 12:00 to 3:00 and 7:00 to 11:00.

La Rotonde, 105, boulevard du Montparnasse (métro Vavin, 6th)

Big changes have come over the years to the small, unassuming café which opened on this spot in 1911. For one, you'd be hard pressed these days to find an understanding proprietor willing to run a tab for or forgive the debts of poor artists and writers. When subsequent owners transformed it into a huge restaurant with a dance hall upstairs, a snootier class of people became the clientele. Perhaps this was the reason La Rotonde was scorned by Hemingway in a Toronto newspaper article as not being a hangout for serious artists. In fact, the bohemian attire he saw on the customers reminded him of the bird house at the zoo! Not all Americans shunned this café, however; far from it. T. S. Eliot and Scott Fitzgerald, for example, often dropped by. Edna St. Vincent Millay and her mother regularly came here for dinner in 1922 when they lived in a hotel just down the street. Lovers found the café to their liking as well. In the 20s photographer Man Ray first saw his future muse and mistress, the French artist's model Kiki de Montparnasse, at this café. A decade later Henry Miller expressed his love for Anaïs Nin who met him every day on the terrace. The Rotonde is open for business daily from 7:30 a.m. to 1:00 a.m.

Le Select, 99, boulevard du Montparnasse (métro Vavin, 14th)

From its beginnings in 1923, this café opposite La Coupole had the distinction of being the first business on the boulevard to stay open all night. Like the Dôme, the awning out front announces that it is an "American Bar" and it didn't take long for many of our country's expatriates to find their way there. They were, in fact, flocking through its doors; only the Wall Street crash of 1929 slowed the flood of Americans to the site. Authors such as Robert McAlmon, Kay Boyle, and Scott Fitzgerald—and later Faulkner and Dos Passos—came here, as did Djuna Barnes and her lover Thelma Wood. Another writer, Henry Miller, often short on funds, came to the Select to scrounge money from friends. He went on to evoke Le Select, along with Le Dôme, in his novel *Tropic of Cancer*. Editor/publisher Margaret Anderson reported that she saw Hemingway every morning at this café, which he celebrated in his novel *The Sun Also Rises*. In July 1929 the Select was the scene of a drunken brawl over a bill between poet Hart Crane and the waiters. You can add your name to the long list of American patrons by dropping in any day during its current hours, 7:00 a.m. to 2:00 a.m. And, just maybe, if you are a fan of ham and cheese sandwiches *à la francaise*, you'll agree with actor/comedian Bill Murray that they make the best *croque monsieur* in town!

In Saint-Germain:
Brasserie Lipp, at 151, boulevard Saint-Germain (métro Saint-Germain-des-Prés, 6th)

Opposite the Flore you'll find this legendary and quite charming restaurant. Its founder Léonard Lipp, who opened for business in 1880, featured specialties from his native region of Alsace. This practice, we are happy to report, continues today with dishes like *choucroute garnie* (sauerkraut served with sausage and pork). In 1926 the brasserie was redone in the Art Deco style and has since achieved historical monument status for its mosaics, tiles, and paintings. The warm, welcoming atmosphere attracts many present-day tourists, but in earlier times it was a favorite of the international artistic, literary, and political elite—think Picasso, Proust, and former French President François Mitterrand. A long list of American writers— from Hemingway to Kay Boyle, Sherwood Anderson, and Archibald

MacLeish in the 1920s, Dorothy Parker in the '30s, James Baldwin and Richard Wright in the 1940s-50s—figure among the many past patrons. Culinary idol Julia Child and her husband used to drop by for dessert in the years they lived in Paris after World War II. You might want to indulge in something sweet yourself…baba au rhum, perhaps, or one of their famous *millefeuilles* pastries, which we refer to as Napoleons. Expect to pay the price for whatever you get, of course, which is probably a little more suitable for Cheapos' wallets at lunch rather than at dinnertime. Brasserie Lipp is open from 11:45 a.m. to 12:45 a.m.

Les Deux Magots, 6, place Saint-Germain des Prés (métro Saint-Germain-des-Prés, 6th)

Ever wonder how this place got its quirky name? Well, walking in, you can't miss the two large Asian figurines on the wall and "magots" apparently refers to stocky figures from the Far East. They were installed by a previous shop owner to indicate that customers could purchase silk lingerie from China there. After the café was established here, the statues stayed where they were and even got the place named for them. With its great terrace and prominent position on the place Saint-Germain, Les Deux Magots is still quite the hit with modern-day tourists…if not so much with Parisians. But it once served as the number one rendezvous for an international group of artists, intellectuals, and literary types. Picasso came here, as did Camus and Sartre (more than likely not together), Oscar Wilde, and James Joyce. It was quite popular with American writers, too—from writers like Baldwin and Wright, to Hart Crane, Lawrence Ferlinghetti, and Archie MacLeish. Longtime Paris resident and *New Yorker* journalist Janet Flanner regularly dropped by for breakfast and at times had serious discussions with Hemingway at a quiet table in the back. In the early 1970s singer Jim Morrison and his girlfriend patronized the café. With all of these bohemian types around, it seems appropriate that the owners created a major prize in 1933 to honor off-beat literary works largely ignored by the Prix Goncourt. Les Deux Magots is open from 7:30 a.m. to 1:00 a.m. daily.

Le Café de Flore, 172, boulevard Saint-Germain (métro Saint-Germain-des-Prés, 6ᵗʰ)

Some places deserve to be labeled an institution. One of the oldest cafés in Paris, the Flore has got it all: food and drink, albeit at high prices, a great Left Bank location, a fine terrace for people watching, as well as being historically significant. It was popular with writers and artists during the First World War, but really hit its stride in the years surrounding World War II. French intellectuals Sartre and Beauvoir came to discuss existentialism with Camus and spent so much of their day here that it was like their second home. If those red leather benches could talk, they would also mention all of the Americans they have accommodated over the years. Authors from Richard Wright to Truman Capote came here, as did The Doors front man Jim Morrison. In the early 50s James Baldwin revised much of his semi-autobiographical novel, *Go Tell It on the Mountain,* upstairs. Even recent and contemporary writers such as Susan Sontag and Douglas Kennedy sat at this café's tables to do their work. Adding to its sterling reputation, a literary prize named for the Flore was created in 1994 to honor the best young French-language writers the world over. The café is currently open for business every day and part of the night from 7:30 a.m. to 1:30 a.m. And, who knows? You might just catch sight of a celebrity or two, such as Johnny Depp or Jack Nicholson.

La Palette, 43, rue de Seine (métro Mabillon or Saint-Germain-des-Prés, 6ᵗʰ)

It pays to know your clientele. And when your café is situated four minutes away from the École des Beaux-Arts (National School of Fine Arts), you should expect an artistic crowd and maybe choose an appropriate name, decorate the walls with paintings, and even hang a framed artist's palette above the bar. Check. Since its opening in 1905, this café-restaurant has been doing all of that and in the process has been welcoming some pretty well-known painters—the likes of Cézanne, Braque, and Picasso. Writers, too, patronized this smaller spot located off the beaten track in Saint-Germain. Hemingway naturally found his way here. In the mid-twentieth century, though, La Palette veered a bit off course and became a major center for drug deals. Beat Hotel resident, novelist, and avowed junkie Bill Burroughs might have even peddled opium here, though French police could never catch him in the act. In the early 1970s it was a favorite of the "rock poet" Jim Morrison. In fact, Morrison might have spent part of the day he died at La Palette. Today the hip wine bar is apparently drug free and boasts a beautifully preserved art deco back room which was declared a historical monument in 1984. Drop by for a beverage any time between 8:00 a.m. and 2:00 a.m. or for a bite to eat during restaurant hours from noon to 3:00 p.m. And you might just spot Harrison Ford or Julia Roberts!

Le Procope, 13, rue de l'Ancienne Comédie (métro Odéon, 6th)

Talk about old! Nestled between the boulevard Saint-Germain and the rue Saint-André des Arts, this restaurant has been around since 1686. So, if you would like a big dollop of history with your *coq au vin* or steak-frites, this is the place for you. Notable figures from the past who used to gather here include French Enlightenment writers Voltaire and Rousseau around the time of the French Revolution. Inside a glass case on the premises is a hat supposedly from a young officer named Napoleon Bonaparte who, it is claimed, left it as collateral when he couldn't pay the tab. American Founding Fathers were well represented here as well. In these surroundings in 1778 Benjamin Franklin worked on the Treaty of Alliance which assured French military help during the American Revolution. Another regular, Thomas Jefferson, spent time here and may have even composed letters home which helped shape the U.S. Constitution. In the 1830s Oliver Wendell Holmes, Sr. and his fellow medical students from

Boston used to drop by while taking a break from classes at a local hospital. Over a century later authors such as Dick Wright continued the habit of patronizing Le Procope. Nowadays the restaurant is open daily from noon to midnight. Some recent tourists who have hit it right have been invited in by the waitstaff for photo-ops before the evening meal service. Cheapos and Snobs alike should try their luck for a peek at the original Parisian "literary café"!

Le Tournon, 18, rue de Tournon (métro Odéon, 6th)

Tucked away near the north side of the Jardin du Luxembourg is a modern-day wine bar specializing in traditional French cuisine. Current customers include journalists, celebrities, and politicians from the nearby French Senate. Back in the late 1940s and early 50s, though, it was a simple, cozy place where customers lingered for hours over a favorite beverage, while playing chess or smoking their plant of choice. Many expats knew it as "Dick's place" because novelist Richard Wright, who lived just a few streets away on the rue Monsieur-le-Prince, dropped in most every afternoon after lunch. He would buy a cup of coffee and visit with friends like mystery writer Chester Himes and French intellectuals Sartre and Beauvoir. But the real attraction for Wright was the pinball machine—a very rare sight in the capital in those days. Writer James Baldwin also dropped in occasionally but found the crowd largely unsympathetic to gays. The Tournon stage was the scene of musical history: Duke Ellington, Billy Strayhorn, and some fellow band members introduced café patrons to jazz at this very spot. The staff of *The Paris Review*, including founding editors George Plimpton and Peter Matthiessen, used to walk over from their office around the corner on the rue Garancière. The Tournon is open from 7:30 a.m. (8:00 on Saturday) till midnight every day except Sundays when it is closed.

Conclusion

ON A TRIP ABROAD in 1934 baseball's Sultan of Swat George Herman Ruth complained that "Paris ain't much of a town." Of course, this comment says more about the Bambino—who was disappointed at not being recognized for the big star he was—than it does about the French capital. There was a time, however, a century or so earlier when Babe Ruth would have been right on target. As late as the mid-1800s, Paris—dark, crowded, unhealthy, and medieval—was viewed as London's shabby neighbor. An immense revitalization project—commanded by Emperor Napoleon III, nephew of Bonaparte, and carried out by city prefect Georges-Eugène Haussmann—brought light, air, and, shall we say, class into malodorous and sickly areas of downtown via wide boulevards and magnificent architecture. You could say that this guidebook has, at least in part, the purpose of proving Babe Ruth wrong. For, it is not for nothing that Paris has long been and remains one of the top tourist destinations in the world.

For most of us of the Snob persuasion, *la belle ville* certainly fills the bill: a feast for the eyes and the palate as well. And, while expensive, Paris can cost a lot less than other world capitals such as London or New York…if Cheapos play their cards right. Well-chosen lodgings, cafés, restaurants, and even food trucks provide the discerning traveler with an affordable visit. Another equally important smorgasbord is to be found in the number of offerings which enrich the mind and the soul. Observing the outstanding beauty of Notre-Dame and the Eiffel Tower (at least from down below) is free for the taking. The Louvre, the Musée d'Orsay, the Cluny, and the Rodin Museum might set you back a few euros but will have you staring in awe at their collections of art. Besides all of the main attractions, discussed in Chapter 3, many options—such as parks, panoramas, and even cemeteries—are well worth the trip and won't set you back a single *centime*.

In addition, genuine Cheapo Snobs, by way of this guide, can get to know the French capital by exploring addresses associated with famous Americans. You're really in luck there, because, usually for the simple cost of a subway or bus ticket, you can visit the streets and quiet neighborhoods where a variety of our writers, politicians, artists and architects, musicians and performers lived, worked or played. As we have seen, many of our nation's greatest—from Hemingway, Fitzgerald, and company to Buchwald and Flanner, Franklin and Jefferson, Calder and Sargent, Gershwin and Morrison, to name a few—chose Paris as their part-time home out of all the cities in the world. Following in their footsteps is indeed a dream come true for anyone proud to wear the label of Cheapo Snob. So, get to work! Plan your itinerary. Include some famous bars and cafés and have the time of your life. Bon voyage!

Acknowledgments

Two PEOPLE ARE DESERVING of special recognition: my son Daniel who gave me both the name Cheapo Snob and the idea to write a guidebook to Paris; Eloise Brière, my professor and friend, who suggested I research where famous Americans had lived in the French capital. There would be no book without them. I also appreciate my son Alex's contribution in setting up websites to accompany the book. And I would like to express my gratitude to my friend Julie Restuccia for proof-reading the final manuscript. So many friends and family members have encouraged and helped me along the way and I thank them all.

30718774R00112

Made in the USA
Columbia, SC
29 October 2018